THERE'S MORE TO ME

Living With MS

EMMIE STATHOPOULOS

INTRODUCTION

"One day, you'll tell your story.
Of how you've overcome what you're going through now,
And it will become part
Of someone else's survival guide"
..... Brene Brown

In 1999, I found out I had Multiple Sclerosis. Not surprisingly, I went through as many books as I could find on the subject, read about how some people cured themselves, the different diets, the different medical options, the traditional and not traditional methods etc. I sought out private practitioners and even tried self-healing.

I went through all the stages of emotional responses starting with the most obvious, denial. And after 20+ years of not (*yet*) finding a cure, (or relief at the very least), I am now trying hypnosis, grief management, re-trying reiki, plus a few more things.

It is because of, and due to this therapeutic journey, that I started writing this book. At first, I was simply putting on paper the thoughts and memories which trickled, and which later flowed (and flooded) my mind. The thoughts continued pouring in, and I found myself wanting to write more and more. In doing so, I discovered how much anger I had stored in me, and how little I understood the meaning of certain events and different experiences. And while I am still working on acceptance, I found out that I have debilitating fears.

> I have learned that when sadness comes to visit me, all I can do is say "I see you." I spend some time with it, get up, and say goodbye.
> I don't push it away, I own it.
> And because I own it, I let it go.
> - Carolina Zacaria -

I have been through *stuff*. Remembering and refacing them all was not easy. But I wanted to. I had to write this book; if nothing else, I knew I would find peace of mind.

It is time to tell my story.

PART ONE ...

"When you are healthy, you have a million wishes.
When you are sick, you only have one wish,
to be healthy again."
..... Ed Sheeran

CHAPTER 1

Who I am, where I came from

My story. The story of me, my life (or lack of), living and coping with MS. The story of who I was, what I was, who I have become, and more. If I can help other MS sufferers (survivors), I am pleased. At the very least, I am telling my story and hope that someone will find a positive message.

You will discover (soon enough) that I am not a professional writer. This book is by no means a literary masterpiece. This book is a result of therapy. It is a compilation of my thoughts and actual experiences. And with that explanation, I welcome you into my mind. Be fore-warned, it is going to be a bumpy, emotional, revealing, and scary ride. And at times, it will be ugly.

Although I was christened *Mary Ellen*, I go by the name Emmie. I will explain that later. I am 57 years old. And I will be 57 until I hit 70, at which time I will be 63. That's my math and I'm sticking to it. Of course, my friend Marie knows exactly what I mean since she and I calculate our age the same way. Marie and I have been friends since we were 8 years old. And at 57 ☺ we are still going strong.

Before I get to the explanation of *Mary Ellen*, I want to introduce you to my parents.

My mother Catherine, *Ekaterini*.

Katy to her friends. My mother was born in Crete, one of Greece's most beautiful islands. She came to Canada at the beginning of the 1950s. She had quite the journey. I say *had* because she died in 2015. She suffered with and struggled with dementia.

Mom was born in a small village on the isle of Crete. She was possibly one of the smartest and most determined women I have ever known. Mom was the second born to my grandparents Maria and Dimitri (aka James in North America).

My grandmother, as my mother has told me, was a stunningly beautiful woman. Very much so. When yiayia (grandma) Maria was in grade 3, she was expelled from school because her beauty was a '*distraction to the boys*'. She must have been a beautiful child too.

My papou (grandfather) Dimitri was what I imagine would today be the equivalent to an city councilor. I don't know how they met, but I know my grandmother was 27 when they got married. I do not know how old my grandfather was. Mom heard stories from my grandmother that her Dimitri was a wonderful husband. Yiayia had told mom, that when the political party he represented was in power, they lived well. But when the elections went the other way, they suffered financially.

On Sundays, when Dimitri was home, he wouldn't let my grand-mother do any housework. He would take over. When the village women said anything or tried to shame my grandmother, he would step in and tell them in no uncertain terms, that his wife worked hard at maintaining cleanliness 6 days a week. He believed strongly that when he was home, she would rest! Wow! Too bad he wasn't there to protect my grandmother when she was permanently expelled from school.

Mom barely remembers her father. He died of pneumonia before her second birthday. She had an older brother, Leonida (Leonard in North America), who became the father figure in her life - unfortu-nately, for a very brief period. From timelines I have pieced together, Leonida was born in 1920. My mom came by 8 years later.

Hmmm. I just realized Star Trek's two main characters shared the names of my grandfather and uncle. Cute!

My mother loved her brother. He was superbly handsome. She had only one photo of him which she brought with her when she emigrated to Canada. It is now in my possession. She also brought with her an old dictionary (Greek to English / English to Greek) which belonged to her brother. Those were the only two things she had of her brother.

I remember that dictionary. It was always by her side. It was her trea-sure. It was all she had that had belonged to him, and it was never out of her sight. The cover was a thin leather. The pages had tiny print and were rice paper thin. They were sepia in colour, and the print was in the same brown tone as was the cover. This little dictionary was 3 x 5, but to my mother it was her world. I am now sorry I didn't hang on to that dictionary when my mom's house was cleared after her death.

My father and mother were having a heated argument one day. (They argued, a lot.) My father took mom's dictionary and threw it across the room. The book spine broke, and some page sections came loose. Mom immediately went and got it. She also spewed several well selected adverbs and adjectives towards my father. She was beyond angry, beyond outraged. Of this I am certain, because until this incident, I had never heard my mother swear. I did not even realize my mother knew how to swear. In any language - (and she could converse in 4 languages). I never heard her swear like that, ever again.

Back to the dictionary, she used a needle and thread and put her beloved brother's dictionary back together. She held the cover together with masking tape.

They say with every fight, a piece of the couple's togetherness gets destroyed. The tape may have held the dictionary together, but it would have taken a container full of tape to reunite my parents. I wonder sometimes if my father knew how much damage that outburst caused; and (frankly) whether he cared.

In my eyes, my yiayia Maria (Mary), was a formidable woman. When my grandfather died, far too early, she was left completely alone to bring up their two children. No welfare, no government subsidies, no widow's pension, no education, and no job. (As if she could leave a 2-year-old and work outside the house). She lived in the house my grandfather had built, no indoor plumbing, no electricity. But she did it. She made it work. And I am in total awe of her. From what

I understand, she did laundry and odd chores for neighbours in exchange for food to feed her children, and herself.

WWII came. History tells us that the German forces were met with extreme resistance in their attempt to occupy Greece, especially the isle of Crete. To demonstrate superiority, and to punish the citizens for their defense/defiance, the German army posted on Crete gathered all the men of my mom's village (men who were too young or too old to be serving in the Greek army), and they shot them dead, executed them in the public square.

My mom did not witness the executions, but my grandmother did. Her son was executed in front of her. What horror! Her firstborn child, her son, gone! From that day on she wore nothing but black. Mom said that my grandmother drenched everything in the house in black, including the sheets and pillowcases. Understandably it scared my mother, and she hated the colour black for years and years.

EVERY WOMAN
WHO HEALS HERSELF,
HEALS ALL THE WOMEN
WHO CAME BEFORE HER
AND ALL THE WOMEN
WHO COME AFTER HER

Why am I telling you about my maternal grandmother (and soon I will tell you about my mother)? Because I share the DNA of these two ladies. I share their memories, curses and patterns. Their memories molded my life. Want it or not, like it or not, my life is a result of, and/or continuation of theirs.

My mother and grandmother struggled during the German occupation. They were rationed food. Mom remembers being given a handwritten ticket allocating her and my grandmother to 3 kilos of potatoes. She heard my grandmother say that would not be enough to get them through the winter. Having seen the concern in my grandmother's face, mom changed the 3 to an 8. She knew if what she had done was discovered, she would have been executed on the spot. She did it anyway, and although she was scared, she didn't show it.

Fast forward 5 horrible years ... the war had ended. Left behind was poverty, destruction, and devastation. My mom realized that she had to do something to support herself and her mother. So, she left for Athens. She did not want to leave her mother to deal with life by herself and completely alone, but she knew she had no other option. She had to help, whatever that took. Singlehandedly, she put herself through dressmaking school. She worked and not only supported herself, but with every pay, she sent money to Crete to support her mother.

Mom ACED her exams. She was a natural. She could even create her own patterns. I remember seeing her graduation certificate. The red seal, and *100%* in large font. Her photo was next to the seal. I remember when looking at it, I saw a very young mom, I remember thinking how beautiful she was, and how talented. I don't know what happened to that framed certificate or where it is now. Maybe my sister has it.

In Greece at the time, (and I imagine in other European cities), good dressmakers lived in the home of the family for whom they sewed. They were live-ins. My mother was hired by and lived with the family of a bank manager. I remember hearing the family name. For reasons of privacy, I will just refer to them as Family K. Mom loved and respected the lady of the house. Mrs. K. became my mother's mentor and had a huge impact on her life. Mom often spoke of the time spent with this family, and of the wise teachings she received there.

Since my mother lived at the home of Family K., she had no expenses for room and board. She would send money to my grandmother and save the rest for her future, or as she would then refer to it, for rainy days.

Life went on. Like her mom, mom too was a very attractive woman. She made friends. And she caught the eye of many men. But she did not pay any attention to them or get swayed by anything that would alter her plans. She grew up relying only on herself, loving her family (dead and alive), respecting her folklore, and listening carefully to the advice and teachings of Mrs. K.

I do not know all of what was said, but I say without doubt, this woman had a huge impact on my mother's life.

Canada opened its borders to workers, specifically manual labourers. Mom found out that maids were high in demand. She decided she was going to emigrate. She was going to work for a few years, make her fortune, and return to her beloved homeland, (the dream of thousands at the time.) And so, she filed her application, and to make her case more convincing, in the evenings she would be found in the homes of her friends, where she would wash their dishes so that her hands would get rough. She would have and show immigration officials, the hands of a maid.

Earlier, I told you my mother could converse in 4 languages. Greek of course was her mother tongue. She understood German, which she learned during the war. But before coming to Canada she taught herself a few words in English. Then when here, she took English and French courses.

In the 50s, the government did not pay for language courses for immigrants; mom worked and put herself through these courses.

She had total commitment and she successfully learned French and English. And when she worked in the factories, she learned Italian from the workers there. She had a knack for learning languages. And the apple did not fall far from the tree. ☺

My father Michael (Mihali)

Mike to everyone he knew. Dad was the third of seven children. He had an older brother, a sister (who never saw her first birthday), and was followed by a brother, a sister, and two more bothers, one of which died a crib death.

My father was a mischievous little boy who was excellent at thinking up ingenious ways to get into trouble. He was quite the handful who was so intelligent, that his boredom bred his mischief. The things he concocted were amazing, and the pranks he played were amazingly funny. Dad was the original MacGyver. I remember one of his coworkers telling my mother (in awe), that if dad had free reign and resources, he would successfully make robots!

Dad was the go-to person amongst my parent's friends. It did not matter if someone needed mechanical, electrical, plumbing (etc.) help. Dad was the person they called.

My father was barely 16½ when he was conscripted, forced to fight for his country. If you recall reading earlier, he had an older sister who had died a crib death. The town records erroneously showed the second born Stathopoulos was of conscription age. In actuality though, dad was the 3rd born. He should have been spared. *And yet........*During his time as a soldier, there were a number of life-threatening close calls, thankfully he survived.

> *The town records showed a 'Michael' Stathopoulos as the 3rd born. Years later, every time my dad visited Greece, he had issues. In Greece, it is mandatory for boys to serve 2 years in the armed forces. The officials were seeking the Michael Stathopoulos who did not serve.*

When the war ended, despite the poverty and depression in Greece, dad found a job. He worked hard.

My grandfather Panagiotis (Peter for the non-Greek speaking readers) was manager at a hotel. With so many kids, his wife, yiayia Eleni (Ellen) stayed home and raised them. Very few mothers worked back then. Money was tight. The house they rented (where dad was born), is where my grandmother lived out her remaining years.

Yiayia Eleni had a special gift. She communicated with the dead. She saw entities. She did not see them as dead. She saw them and spoke with them as you and I see and speak with friends and neighbours. From stories I have heard from my dad, others on her side of the family had similar gifts, although not to the same extent.

Dad told me that one of her brothers – my great uncle – freed the spirit of a murdered soldier who was plastered in the wall of the home in which he lived. Seemingly my great uncle got a message from the dead soldier one night, in a dream.

My grandmother's sightings and visitations on the other hand were much more elaborate, much more realistic. And apart from another brother's goodbye message (as he was dying), many of the messages my grandmother received were of a healing nature. She saved her daughter's life by doing what a spirit (or entity) told her to do. Saving the baby even shocked the local doctor who had told my grandparents that the baby was not expected to survive the night. The doctor went to the house the next morning expecting to sign a death certificate. What he found was a miracle.

I do not know for sure what the baby had. From my father's description, I suspect she had the whooping cough, it was fatal. During the night, my grandmother saw and greeted someone named *Mrs. Marina*, someone only she could see and hear. Yiayia Eleni sat in the kitchen with this lady and made her Greek coffee. My grandfather heard my grandma talking (to herself) and just ignored her. He was used to her 'visitations'.

When Mrs. Marina (my grandmother's visitor) left, my grandmother woke my grandfather and told him what he had to do, what he had to get so they could save the baby. Dad told me the story (years later), about the events that took place that night. He knew the events first-hand, since he was the one who accompanied my grandfather on this mission to save the baby. He remembered the details vividly.

When my grandfather woke dad, he briefed him on my grand-mother's visit and the task at hand. Dad did not question any of it. Everyone in the house was used to yiayia's 'visitors'. My dad and my grandfather were to go to a nearby farm and bring back fresh cow dung. Dad told me he recalled the feel of the heat of the fresh dung emitting through the newspaper he used to wrap it.

My grandfather was stressed. He kept telling my dad that if the baby died, he was afraid my grandmother would go crazy. She had lost a baby daughter years before. He told my father that they had to go along with the message yiayia received from her visitor, to minimize the possible horror that was looming. When they got to the house and my grandfather gave my grandmother the newspaper, my grand-mother put the dung in a frying pan and proceeded to fry it. She had been *instructed* to do so.

Once heated, she put the dung on the baby's chest and back. Within minutes, the baby started coughing up gobs of phlegm. I remember my dad acting out how my grandfather put his finger in the baby's mouth to pull out the phlegm. The baby was saved. And that baby, my aunt, was named Marina, after the visitor whose instructions were given to my grandmother that night.

As a little girl, I used to see spirits and talk to them. And
whereas my mother dismissed, ignored, and discouraged me

of speaking about it, my father was convinced I had inherited
some of my grandmother's ability to see spirits.

My father was an absolute wizard in math, in physics, and in reading engineers' drawings. He had 2 patents which were handed over to the government agency/factory for which he worked (while in Greece). In Canada he worked for major companies like Pratt and Whitney, Rolls Royce, Canadair, and Lucas Rotax. But what amazing talents he had in the sciences, he lacked in languages.

It did not take long for his employers to recognize his strengths. The engineers would bring him sketches and drawings and before dad produced the prototypes; he would show them what would or would not work, and why. Oh, by the way, guess who inherited the ability to read a drawing 😊

Like my mom he also came to Canada in the early 1950s. And like my mother, he crossed the Atlantic on the Queen Mary. He landed in Halifax with just under $60 in his pocket, and from there he took the train to Montreal. It was winter and there was snow everywhere. He told me he had to wait until the spring to find out of what the streets and sidewalks were constructed.

Dad did not speak French or English. People from the Greek Community/Greek Orthodox church found him a room and a job. His first job was with Pratt and Whitney. He lived in a room near The Holy Trinity Church (centre of Montreal) and worked in Longueuil, I would say about 20 kms away. On good days he would walk, to save the 15-cent bus fare. And that was probably the last time my father saved money.

Mom had taken a room with a Russian family who lived on St. Urbain, now known as part of the McGill ghetto. They loved her and adopted her (so to speak) as part of their family. I still remember the matriarch and patriarch of that family, Nanny and Papa. Their family was part of our family for decades.

Papa's funeral was the first funeral I attended. I do not think I was in school yet. Nanny died 15 years later.

Through the Greek Community, mom and dad were introduced to each other. My father took one look at my mother and recognized her immediately. It turns out they were neighbours in Faliron, a suburb of Athens, where my father lived, and my mother worked. Dad had seen her on several occasions, but never spoke to her. When my parents announced their engagement, Yiayia Eleni came to Canada. She too recognized my mother; my mom did not recognize her. When she was on the mainland in Greece, mom minded her own business. She had an agenda. Men and relationships were not part of that agenda.

Dad had just turned 32, and according to my grandmother, was too young to get married *LOL* ☺. My mom, bless her soul and character, told my grandmother that my dad owed her nothing (translation, they had not been intimate - not that he hadn't tried) and he was free to be a bachelor for as long as he (or my grandmother) wanted. *Good for you mom!*

They got married. To this day I say it was a marriage *...not based on love*. I do not want to judge. I do not know who felt what, but even a blind dog could see they were not in love. They both worked hard. Very hard. And with each paycheck dad sent money home to his mother. My mother's frustration grew, she was getting increasingly upset that she was working hard and doing without, so that Yiayia Eleni would receive her, 'tithe'. Yiayia Eleni had a husband who was working, she was not in need. Mom decided she was going to put an end to it. She was going to force my father to keep money close to home. And that dear reader, is the reason why I was conceived.

CHAPTER 2

Maternity number one

Mom knew that having a child would force my father to take on responsibility for his new family. What she did not know (how could she), was that getting pregnant would make her horribly sick. Whereas she was okay and gaining some weight in the first 3 months, the last 6 months were a nightmare. Her system would not keep anything she ate. She could not keep anything down. She was throwing up constantly, and when there was nothing left in her stomach, she would throw up blood. And that my father got caught up in a labour dispute. A strike. Two desperately needed incomes got obliterated.

Mom was in labour with me for 36 hours. And when I made my appearance, she apologized to my father that I was a girl. 😣 Every Greek man wanted a boy, didn't he -- to carry on his name.

In Greek tradition, the first-born child carries the name of the paternal grandmother or grandfather, depending of course on the sex. (Remember the movie My Big Fat Greek wedding; "This is my cousin Nick, Nick, Nick, Nick and Nickie"). So, following and according to tradition, I should have been named Helen. But my father was not comfortable, knowing that my mother had become an only child, he knew there was no possibility for anyone but her to have a child which would be named after her side of the family. Besides, dad's niece (his sister's daughter) was named Helen, after yiayia Eleni.

> You had nothing to do with your coming into this world. You may have little or nothing to do with your leaving it. But you have almost everything to do with your life while you possess that life.
>
> —Napoleon Hill

Dad wanted to name me Mary, after my maternal grandmother. After some back and forth, they settled on the names of both grandmothers. I was christened Mary Ellen. And that's who I was until grade two. My grade two teacher said that name did not fit me. She took the M from Mary, and the E from Ellen, and I became M-E, Emmie, the name by which i am known today

Apparently, and according to my mother, when I was born, my legs were crooked. She wanted to put me in a cast. I laugh because all babies are born that way. There was nothing wrong with the shape of my legs. My dad knew there was nothing wrong with me. He told her not to worry, no cast was required.

*I had shapely legs. I really did - thanks to 14 years of classical
ballet.*

There was no Medicare when I was born. And my parents did not
have the money to cover the hospital expenses incurred. My dad
could not take me and my mother home. He could not pay the hospital bill. He went to the Greek Community to ask for guidance or help,
but they were useless.

One of his neighbours sent him to a Catholic service. These angels
not only gave him the money to get my mother and me out of the
hospital, but they never asked him to sign anything. They told him
to pay them back when he could.

*Sometimes I wonder how my father managed to make himself
understood. His English was horrible. His French was worse.*

I was not a good eater, but I was a fantastic baby. I slept 23/24 hours.
It was not until much later they discovered the reason I slept so much
was because I was anemic as was my mother while she carried me.
And my mother had her hands full with me. I just would not eat.
And I kept losing weight. Someone told my mom to let me be. That I
would eat (drink milk) when I got hungry enough.

*Ever feel like telling people who do not know what they are
talking about, to shut the hell up.*

At the end of 3 days, my mother had enough and was afraid that I
was slowly starving. She decided to force feed me. It took days but I
finally started drinking properly. And by properly, I am stretching the
inference. Whereas I was supposed to have 3 ounces of milk every 4

hours, I would have 2-3 ounces every 5 or 6 hours. But at least I had stopped losing weight, and I was eating.

CHAPTER 3

Maternity number 2

My poor mother was pregnant, again, one month after giving birth to me. She was not happy. She had a husband who was unemployed, no money, an infant who would not eat (easily), and she was pregnant again. She had no one to turn to for help. I can only imagine her depression and her frustration. I can't even pretend to understand her state of mind. I feel sorry for what she was going through. She was 26 years old and her life was spiraling out of control. She went from living in a home where there was love and money, where she never had to cook or clean, to a life of disappointment, living in dire straits.

Short of getting an abortion (and I'm guessing that's because she couldn't afford it), she tried every which way she could to terminate her pregnancy. And honestly, I wonder how – how my sister was born undamaged. As determined as my mother was to terminate her pregnancy, my sister was just as determined to survive.

Whereas I sympathize with what my mother was facing, I totally disagree that she spoke openly about it years later. My sister and I did not need to hear how unwanted we were. I am really sorry my mother's life was not a bed of roses, but we weren't the cause.

Mom's frustration mounted. And my eating habits amplified her situation. I was 8 and a half months old, I was on semi solids, but I was still difficult to feed. I simply would not eat. I would store the food in my cheeks, like a chipmunk. I do not know if I was being given too much, or if I was not eating fast enough. Whatever it was, it was enough to push my mother over the edge.

I do not remember the event, fortunately; but I do remember my mother telling me. She told me that one day feeding me was impossible. She was so frustrated that I would not eat that she whipped me out of my highchair and onto the floor. She was going to jump on me. I must have sensed something and just managed to squeak out 'mamma'. That brought her out of her trance and saved my life.

Marina (my sister) was born within a half hour. Since it took 36 hours for me to make my appearance, my father figured he had plenty of time to go home, shower, shave, and get back to the hospital with time to spare. Not so. By the time he got back, my mother had already given birth. And once again she apologized for giving birth to a girl ☹.

When my mother went to deliver my sister, I was given to my godparents to take care of me. They must have been wonderful with me. They said I was easy going; I did not fuss or cry or complain in any way at all. They were happy to have me staying with them.

My godparents took me with them to the hospital when they went to visit my mom and the new baby. The people in the ward with my mom were speaking Polish. My godmother says it was a language that caught my attention. I listened for a while and then I looked right at them and started to babble. She laughed wondering if I was trying to imitate them, or if I was pointing out to them that they were speaking a language I could not understand.

My sister was comfortable in the arms of my mother and father. I on the other hand did not want my mother. I do not know why that was. Could or did I feel her frustration? Did I know my father from a previous life? I do not know. I just know that I did not want my mother holding me. I wanted to be in the arms of my father. I remember seeing a photo of me sitting on my mother's lap, crying, with my arms extended towards my father who was taking the photo.

My parents had 2 babies, born in the same year. I was born in January, Marina in December. And we were so completely different. Whereas I slept and did not require much attention, Marina demanded to be fed every 2 hours and suffered colic pains. Whereas I was content to be plopped in front of a TV, Marina needed interaction. Whereas I stayed quietly in my crib, Marina would grab hold of the railings on her crib and shake it until it travelled halfway across the room. And Marina was much stronger than me. Much more solid, much sturdier. She started walking at 9 months. I did not walk until I was almost 14 months. But although I was late, when I started walking, I was very, very solid on my feet. My mother said I hardly ever fell.

At 18 months I could recite the alphabet, I could count to 20 in English French and Greek, and I was completely potty trained. At

24 months I tripped over my grandmother's foot. Yiayia Maria had come to give my mom a hand, my mother needed to return to work, we desperately needed a second income. I tripped over my grandmother's foot and I went headfirst into an old-style cast iron radiator. My forehead split open, and the blooding wouldn't stop.

The trip to the hospital was my first real memory. I remember being held by my mother; she was sitting in the back seat of the police cruiser. I remember the brown and beige blanket in which I was wrapped, and I remember looking up at my mother's teary face. And telling her not to cry because I did not hurt, and I was not scared.

(Calling the police was a free ride to the hospital. calling an ambulance wasn't).

The policeman in the front seat turned around and looked at me. He was surprised at the words that were coming out of a child that young. He started counting to me in French. But his accent was the (Quebec) French Canadian, and different from the French I had heard my mother speak. I commented about his pronunciation. I remember he laughed.

I was brought to the Children's Hospital. After they stitched me up, I stayed in the hospital for observation. The nurses did not have a problem with me. I could talk. I could tell them what I felt or wanted.

My grandmother went back to Greece the following year. I do not know why. I remember hearing that she was not comfortable here. I do not know what that meant, what was or wasn't said. I did not ask. Something told me not to.

PART TWO ...

"One day it clicks.
You realize what's important and what isn't.
You learn to care less about what other people think of
you and more about what you think of yourself. You
realize how far you've come and remember when thought
things were a mess, that you would never recover.
And you smile. You smile because you are proud
of yourself and the person you have become."
.... unknown

CHAPTER 4

Growing up

At 3 years old I was jumping rope, on the sidewalk outside our house. We lived on Clark Street. I jumped rope flawlessly. I had total coordination and strength. My mother said that pedestrians would stop and watch me. They would be in total disbelief at my coordination. But I was timid. If any kids in the neighbourhood gave me grief, I would shy away and close-up. My sister would have none of it though. She would come down off the balcony, go straight to the kid(s) who bullied me, grab hold of them and either punch them or bite them. She had my back. I did not have the physical strength to defend myself, nor did I care to. Eventually I learned to stand up for myself with words. I still do. When I do.

It was a single word that saved me years ago, 'mamma'.

And at about the same age, I became a kleptomaniac, well, sort of. We were not rich, and to make ends meet, my mother rented a room to Greek immigrants. She would also help them find jobs, lodgings and in some cases, a mate. One day one of the young women who stayed with us approached my mother and told her that she was missing a watch (or ring, or necklace). My mother told her not to worry, her jewelry was safe.

Evidently, I would take the lodgers' jewelry and put the pieces atop a suitcase which was under my bed. When asked why I did it, why I took their jewelry, I told them straight out - I wanted to have pretty things for when I grew up. ☺ And whereas I do not remember any of that, I do remember the suitcase. It was brown, had metal corners, burlap like finish and leather straps. The gold-coloured latches were always open. I remember the dots of discoloration.

It was also about at this time that my mother did something wonderful for me. Even though money was extremely tight, my mother wanted Marina and me to have some culture. I have no idea where she got the money, but she managed to put us both in dance classes. Classical ballet. Marina did not like it, but I took to it like a fish to water. And I was good at it.

My mother had her shortcomings, issues, and demons, but she was a wiz with money. That woman managed to take what little income there was and stretch it to amazing limits. She did not squander anything. Old sheets were cut up and were used as kitchen towels (the sides neatly sewn under). They got washed when soiled and then reused. Leftovers were never thrown out. They were skillfully mixed and served as a new meal. She often repeated her mother's favourite sayings, one of which said, 'the best way to control the budget is to properly utilize your food'. An equally important saying was 'people cannot see the bologna sandwich in your stomach, but they can see and judge you on how you're dressed'. Since mom was a dressmaker, she would sew our clothes, so we always looked great.

It is so clear to me now; how unhappy my mother was. And how much she was in over her head. She was thousands of miles away from her mother (whom she loved dearly and missed even more). She had children for whom she could not care for the way she wanted; and she was wasting her talents working in a factory. She lived a meager existence, in a home with furniture that was clean but ugly, there wasn't enough money (although she made it work – she made ends meet, and more); her dreams were being shattered daily, and she was with a man with whom she couldn't communicate. Worse, she was in a loveless marriage. How lonely she must have felt.

My mother came up with a not so brilliant idea. She decided she would leave my father; she would disappear without a word and leave him to take care of me and my sister. In her mind/plan, he would have to go after her and plead with her to return home.

But before leaving she would stack the odds in her favour. I was instructed to take my sister and get into my parents' bed, and when my father came home from work, we were to cry because our mother left...*wow is us*. Of course, she told me where she would be if I needed her, but I couldn't tell a soul.

> *I was NOT happy. I am 10 months older than my sister. I was only 4 years old, and my mother thought it wise, important, and necessary to make me my sister's guardian and responsible for her. Who makes a 4-year-old responsible for a 3-year-old who is stronger in every sense!*

Days went by. And although I imagine dad looked for her, things were going well at home. I for one, did not miss her. Her plan was failing.

She blamed me. She told me it was my fault. I was not doing my part in convincing anyone that I missed her. Seriously mom?

I do not remember how many days later, she came back. I truly do not remember the details of her return. I must have blocked that chapter in my life. I know that she was hiding out at Nanny's house, the Russian family with whom she lived before marrying my father. I imagine Nanny had convinced her to go back home, that what she was doing was not right.

> *Don't get me wrong. My mother may have had a weird way of rearing children, but she wanted the best for us. She wanted us to succeed. My parents always lived in the poorest part of a good neighborhood so we could attend a better school. A school which had a better class of students. And her Greek roots meant strict discipline.*
> *Ridiculously strict.*

This next bit of information floors me every time I think of it. My mother had squirreled away just under $2 thousand dollars. It was in nickels, dimes, and quarters. She took that money and against everyone's financial advice, against my father's threats and arguments, in 1963 she used that money as down payment on a duplex. Truth be told she and my father worked extremely hard to transform that house. Extremely hard! But they did it.

And when my mother started living a little financial relief, she discovered my father owed $10 thousand in gambling debts. She paid that off and never told anyone - but me of course. And despite my dad's lack of work due to constant layoffs and strikes, not only did they not lose the house, but the mortgage was paid off in 15 years instead of 25.

Regardless of everything (else), I have a huge amount of admiration for that woman. I learned so much from her. And I traveled to so many places with her. I respected her and loved her as my mother, sadly I never saw her as a friend. And since I was a shy and private person, I never told anyone what I was feeling. I did not want to. But oh, the places we visited, the shows to which we went, the outings we had. And I thank her every day for all I learned and inherited from her. Of course, she never stopped controlling me (until I stopped letting her).

My dad was the exact opposite. Dad was calm, cool, collected, a real charmer ... and totally irresponsible. Mom pushed for success, dad smoothed out the wrinkles; and did so until the day he died. These two people should have never been together. If we have subsequent lives, I truly hope they get to spend it with someone with whom they find love. For whatever reason he was not an ideal husband, but as a father, he gave tons of emotional support.

I was fortunate enough to be with him when his soul left his body. I feel blessed that he was not alone. I feel cursed because I felt helpless that I could not and didn't do anything to save him.

Grade school was pretty much uneventful, besides the fact that I did 4 schools in 6 years. I am not tooting my horn, but I was good in school. I was not a brainiac, I had to work hard, but I did make the honour role for many years. And how I loved sports and gymnastics. I was quite the tomboy camouflaged in the grace of a ballet dancer. And since I was short and small, a very deceptive physical appearance, I was a surprisingly good athlete.

Mom would *motivate* us by telling us that if we did not get an education, we would end up mopping floors. I spent several sleepless nights worrying about my sister's future because she did not study - when she didn't want to. I was a kid, losing sleep, over a fear instilled in me, for someone and something that was completely out of my control!

My mother ruled with an iron fist when it came to lessons (English, French and Greek). My dad on the other hand was the one who found ways to explain what I could not understand. I remember one night when he stayed up with me until way after midnight, until I finally understood why 3 hundreds and 8 tens, was the same as 38 tens. He did not lose his temper once. I am proud to say that I inherited that patience. Fortunately. So, when my son was in school, when he blocked somewhere, I had the ability to find a way that would help him understand.

High school was fun, especially when I found out I could take Mechanical Drawing. Fun and funny. Not only was I the only girl in that class, but I was the only girl Mr. B had taught in over fifteen years. I still remember him on the very first day. The class was in the basement of our high school. Mr. B. was coming down the stairs, looking over his latest bunch of students. I remember the awkward pause, foot in midair, when he spotted me.

I was independent. I recall how he used to say, "Small Fry" (that's what he called me), "you're going to learn the hard way that most boys and men are going to be intimidated by and resent your intelligence and independence". Damn was he right! That is another chapter though. In a class of males, I was the one who could differentiate between a tap, a drill, and a bore. I could see the cross sections on the front, rear, and side views of plans. I could see which parts of the drawing depicted the solid part of an object, and which did not.

I may have had fun times, but high school was not smooth sailing. I was a cute *kid*, while others around me were *women*. My younger sister had bloomed. I was still a kid. Cute, bright, graceful, but still a kid. And for some reason I still do not understand, my mother found it acceptable to label me *abnormal*, and to laugh about it. Remember all the good advice she got when I was an infant who wouldn't eat? Well, she got more of that wonderful advice from people who told her to hold off taking me to a doctor, to wait. I do not know who it was, who finally told her to seek medical advice. When the doctor confirmed I had all the necessary parts, I was put on a series of hormone injections. Houston, we no longer had a problem.

My grandmother was thrown out of school for being beautiful (developed early). Was my body doing the exact opposite to protect me from something?

Are you still with me? I finished high school and CEGEP and went looking for a temporary or full-time job. I was not ready to go to university yet (I did my degree in communications engineering later). I had part time jobs since I was 14. I was not convinced I was ready to find my official permanent full-time job, I still wanted to go to school, eventually, just not quite yet. I wanted some time off.

One of the summer jobs I had was not supposed to be more than that, a summer job. But by the end of summer, I had been promoted to a position which suddenly became vacant. I did a super job at it. The money and independence were good, so I stayed on. I was making a living. And I was giving my pay to my mother. She in turn gave me an allowance with which I had to make do. She said that my father worked hard for years, it was time for him to take a breather. And since I was working, I had to help.

I didn't know it at the time, but she held on to every penny I gave her. And she gave it all black to me when I got married. All of it.

I remember one job, my *starting* salary was equivalent to what my father was making. And crap, I was not expecting that. The interviewer asked me if I felt I was worth the salary offered. I quickly gave her the right answer. But on the inside, I was wondering if my dad would be proud, or would his ego take a beating. I got the job. And I never told my dad the truth about the salary.

I had many boyfriends, but I never let them get too close. I enjoyed my youth. And while I enjoyed people of my age, I felt most comfortable in the company of older, more seasoned, strong people. My sister and my friends were already married. I had no desire to follow suit. I was more interested (in order or priorities)

1. Dancing
2. Being successful at work
3. Dancing
4. Being in the company of people who had interesting life-experiences
5. Dancing
6. Keeping my independence

I was in my early 20s. Getting married was the last thing I wanted. I had lived with two people who had a marriage that I would not wish on anyone. Several of my boyfriends wanted to marry me. That was my signal to bail.

And then I met my soon to be husband. Physically he was nothing like the Adonis' I used to bring home. As a matter of fact, when I introduced him to my parents, my mother thought I was joking. But I was happy with him. And so, we got married. I was 26. Our happiness lasted 6 months. By month 11, we were divorced. I felt like an absolute failure. To me, it was not a failed marriage. I saw it that it was *me* who was the failure. In my mind, I had just lived something worse than what I saw when I was living at home.

My dad was by my side... not doing anything special. Just there to make sure I was not feeling alone. My mother (bless her heart) asked me if I had done 'enough to keep him'. *Thanks mom.*

We split, and we got divorced. I was left alone to pay for a rent that required 2 paychecks. At that time, I was being paid bi-weekly. And after paying rent, hydro, insurance, phone, I had $15 to last until the next pay period. That meant $15 to cover food, gas, entertainment etc. I went from a size 8 to a size 2 in a very short period. It was simple, I only ate when and what I could. But I made sure that my responsibilities were covered. I was hurt. I felt rejected. And every man who knew me, thought that it was open season on Emmie. *Assholes.*

My ex thought he had left his winter coat behind. And so, he sent me a registered letter claiming $200 for the coat. I couldn't afford to eat and he wanted $200! Really?! Bang! That was a defining moment. I got to fully understand the expression **"seeing red"**. Because that is exactly what I saw. There was blood in my eyes. I wrote him a scathing letter. Within 48 hours I got a call from him, at work, telling me I owed him nothing. And before hanging up he made sure to tell me I was a *beep, beep, beep.*

*Months later I discovered he really had left his coat behind. It was a nice camel coloured wool coat **that I had bought him**. And it looked great on my dad.* 😊

PART THREE ...

"There's something within you that knows what to do.
There's a power greater than you that knows
how to take care of you without your help.
All you've got to do is to surrender to it.
Surrender your thoughts, your mind, your
ego, to the current that knows the way.
It will take care of you.
It will take better care of you than you can ever imagine."-
..... Robert Adams

CHAPTER 5

I can, I will

After all that had happened, I had no use for men, other than the obvious. I immersed all my energy in my job. Fortunately, within a few months, I got offered a job which paid $15K a year more than what I was making. In addition, the job included a bonus plan, a car and expenses. That job offer found me! I was not looking or applying anywhere. One of the VPs had witnessed firsthand how I worked, and he sought me out. My financial anxiety subsided, and my confidence went up.

The job was going well. I was in my late 20s. I was making a fantastic living at a job I loved. It is a job which dealt with (what was then) modern technology. I was in my element. There was something new to learn and teach almost every other month. I was very good at my job and one of the few women in a male dominated position. And I could make heads turn wherever I walked by *LOL*. I was right where I wanted to be...almost. I wanted a baby.

I wanted a baby. I didn't want a husband, nor did I want a part time father to my baby. I just wanted a baby. I recall being in the car with my mother when I told her I wanted a child, only a child. She asked me if I was thinking responsibly or if I was thinking egotistically. Was I being fair to deprive that child of a full family. And what about my career. I was out of town so often. How was I going to balance everything? I do not know if I agreed with her reasoning or if I got scared hearing the veracity of her words. I altered my plans. But not my goal. The goal remained the same.

Luck stepped in. I ran into George, a childhood friend whom I had not seen since he and I had gone on with life, we had both gotten married. It was his birthday, that day that I ran into him. I invited him for a drink. At the time, I was already divorced, and he was in the process of getting one. We hooked up and the rest fell into place.

We lived together for a while. Then we decided to buy a house. We saved until we had enough money to buy a condominium. And one summer we found one we could afford. It was in Laval, in construction phase. (Laval is off the island of Montreal.)

I had the insight to have a clause added to the purchase agreement that if the condo was not ready for delivery on December 1st as promised, I (the buyer) had the option to refuse closing the purchase, and our deposit was to be refunded in full. As the months went by, we occasionally visited the construction site, to check the progress. And each time we visited, I realized more and more that I did not want to cross the bridge to get to Laval. I did not want that condo.

I saw an ad in the paper for a new townhouse development in Pointe-Claire (the west island part of Montreal). I convinced my boyfriend for us to go look. Whereas he would have normally refused, (after all, we had already bought a condominium), he agreed to go look. I suspect he too did not relish having to cross the bridge, at the very least twice a day. So, we went to look at this new development being advertised.

I immediately fell in love with the model home. We both did. But what little money we had, had been used for the deposit/down payment on the condo. Furthermore, we would still be short by $45,000. We would not be able to meet the requirement of the deposit for the townhouse.

I did some calculations. By the look of things, the condo would not be ready for December 1st. I would be able to recoup our deposit. And we could sell our cars, both of us. Which was a real commitment from George. His car was his passion. It was a muscle car he had spent months restoring. We were going to rely on the leased car that came with his job. But rats, we would still be short $15,000. Oh well, instead purchasing an end unit we would buy a middle unit. The middle unit was exactly $15,000 less expensive.

My parents helped. In reality, it was my mom who stepped in. She said she would lend us the balance required so that we could buy the end unit we really wanted. And we could take up to 20 years to pay her back.

I found out later, my mother had no intention of taking the $15,000 back, she just never said anything at the time.

So, with the help of my parents, we bought our house. I crunched the numbers again; we were just going to make it. No room for anything else. No wiggle room at all. The memory of my mother buying their duplex came to mind. No wiggle room. On the day we were scheduled to sign for the mortgage, I discovered I was pregnant. *Yippee* on the pregnancy, and *yikes* on the mortgage payments.

Fast forward...I was 8 months pregnant when we took possession of the house. We weren't in it one week; I was at work when I got a call from my boyfriend (now my husband), to tell me the company with which he was employed would be closing *in 2 days*! Gone would be the badly needed 2nd income and gone would be our only car. We needed to find wheels (we could not afford), and fast. My dad found us a $200 beater. And when I say beater, I am not kidding. We could not even wash that car; the paint would rinse off with the soap.

I had the baby a month later. And 5 days after that, I had what I know today - was MS' first calling card, my first symptom.

I was at home. I remember sitting quietly, the baby was in his bassinet. I felt the whole left side of my body go numb. The entire left side. It was as if someone had carved out and split my body in two. The left side of my face, my left eye, left side of my nose, my left ear, my arm and hand, my left leg and foot; they were all completely numb. The numbness lasted seconds or was it minutes. Whatever the duration, it felt so unfamiliar, strange, and scary!

Three weeks later I was in the office of my OBGYN. A standard follow-up, to make sure everything was back where it was supposed to be. I told him about the numbness, and he sent me straight to the neurologist. (both my OBGYN and the neurologist have offices in the same hospital/building). The neurologist checked me, made me jump up and down, checked my balance, my eyes, and my strength and resistance. He did not see anything alarming, so he sent me home.

Time does not stand still. A year and a half later my husband was still out of work. And as much as I appreciated not having to pay for or use daycare, the pressure of being alone to carry the financial burdens was getting unbearable. Still, I would not give in. My mother and grandmother dealt with much worse. I could and would make things work. I was determined to continue, to make ends meet and find a way to a solution.

Fast forward again. My son was 4 years old. My husband was now working...and bang, I lost my job. I was devastated but not defeated. While I actively looked for work, I had time. I took my son to any activity that was free. Thankfully, his swimming lessons were already paid for. And just as thankfully, all activities at the library were free.

Looking back today, I realize how blessed I was to be off work, because I got to spend so much quality time with my son.

One day we walked to the shopping centre. It was not far from home, a good 15-minute walk. Not the safest walk though. We had to contend with areas which were not exactly pedestrian friendly. Whereas he never asked for anything, GM, my 4-year-old son stopped at the window of a jewelry store and stared at a ring. I saw the raw passion and his excitement as he pointed the ring out to me. I could not afford it, but I could not and would not let him down. I put the ring on lay away and tried to figure out how I was going to pay for it.

I decided to start painting. I was pretty good at it, so I painted canvasses and sold them. Sales of my paintings paid for the ring, and I made enough money to supplement the household income.

I remember the first art auction at which my paintings were displayed and were up for sale. I hosted so many emotions, excitement, trepidation, anxiety, and embarrassment. I felt my paintings were like cartoon drawings compared to some gorgeous pieces there. But I did well. I sold all three pieces I was displaying.

Fast forward once more. Six years later we were back on our feet. We both had jobs and things at our house were good. My mother and father on the other hand were barely talking to each other. It was late afternoon that I got a call from the hospital. My father had suffered a heart attack. The hospital had been trying to reach my mother, but they could not find her.

I rushed to the hospital. My dad was visibly shaken and scared. The cardiologist who saw him told us that he would require bypass surgery. Dad did not know what to do and he turned to me. I spoke to the attending cardiologist who told me that whereas there were no guarantees with the surgery, not having the operation meant dad could die at any time.

I tried reaching my mother. I called every half hour, for hours. Finally, at half passed midnight she answered the phone with a very sarcastic and nasty comment. I replied with equal distain and told her that 'her husband' was in the hospital. I was not nice at all. My father was hurting, and she was being a *bitch*.

Today, I wonder if she was really that callous, or if her dementia had started.

Like my grandmother, my father had a heart mummer (I do too). Dad had his own cardiologist. I called him. He was not available. The poor man was in the hospital, a patient himself, fighting cancer. I went to his hospital bed. I identified myself (not having realized that he had already recognized me even though he had not seen me in over 15 years). I told him what had happened to dad and what was happening.

This man was dad's cardiologist, but he was also his friend. The two had been friends for 25 years. I continued telling him about the options presented to dad. He frowned; knowing my dad, and medically following him for a number of years, his suggestion was that my father *does not opt* for the surgery. We talked for a while and I bid him goodbye, both of us knowing that we would probably not see each other.

I went straight to my dad and told him what his friend/cardiologist said. Dad asked me what I thought he should do, what as my opinion. I did not want to give him one, I did not want to make that decision. I did not want to make the wrong choice. I told dad the decision would have to be his. Dad finally, fearfully, and fatefully opted to have the operation.

The day of the operation, I did not leave the hospital. My mother was there until dad was wheeled into the operating room. She said she would return when the operation was done. I could not leave. I did not want to leave. I was not going to leave him alone. And as they were wheeling him into the operating room, he looked at me and told me to look after my mother. The *"if I don't make it"* was implied.

The operation took 3 ½ hours, much longer than scheduled. When it was over, I tracked down the surgeon. I wanted to know what he had to say. He told me that had he known how calcified my father's aorta was, he would not have agreed to perform the operation. My first thought was *then why the hell didn't you stop*.

CHAPTER 6

MS comes calling - again.

It was a day or two later. My dad's operation was over, and he was in ICU. And I fell. My ankle gave out. No rhyme, no reason. I fell, and as I found out later, had broken my foot.

On that day, I had finished work early. I picked up my son from daycare and took him to the park. After a while, it was time to head home and prepare supper etc., and then head to the hospital to see my dad. But on my way from the park to the parking lot, I fell. My ankle gave out. I remember pushing off my foot when I felt myself falling, trying to prevent the fall. I also remember looking around to see if I had stepped on something which might have caused me to lose balance. There was nothing there.

I hobbled to the car. Fortunately, it was my left foot that I just injured, so I could drive. By the time my son and I reached home though, my foot had swollen, and it was throbbing. GeorgeMichael ran into the house I thought to get his dad; but he ran back out with a frozen bag of peas for me to put on my foot (bless his heart).

I was convinced it had suffered nothing more than a sprain and that all I needed was to ice my foot. My husband though was not convinced. He wanted confirmation that my insistence of it being a sprain, was actual. He insisted we go to emergency at our local hospital. At triage, I kept telling the nurse that it was just a sprain. I wanted to get out of there. My dad was expecting me.

When my turn came and I saw the doctor, I told her too that it was just a sprain. She looked at my foot, looked at me, and then pushed on my foot with her thumb. *Hells bells!* I saw stars. It clearly was not just a sprain. I was sent to get my foot x-rayed.

> *George said when the doctor pushed down on my foot, I jumped out of the seat, pushed her hand away and asked her if anyone had hit her yet that day. He had to stifle a laugh. He said I also called her a b**** under my breath. He knew for me to react that way, it had to have really HURT.*

The foot was in fact broken. I was fitted with a walking cast and was told not to take more than a couple of steps on the cast for the next 24 hours. The cast had to dry properly. After that wait time, 24 hours later, I went back to the regular schedule/routine; I went to work, came back home, prepared supper - then headed to the hospital to sit with dad by his bed. The walking cast slowed me down a bit, but it did not stop me. I used a backpack as a purse. With a crutch in one hand and my walking cast. I did not have any issues.

At the hospital. dad would doze off around 9:30 in the evening. Every so often he would wake and glance my way to see if I was still there. By 11:00 pm, when I was sure he was in a deep sleep, I would leave. I did this for months. Fortunately, the cast was not on that long.

Being in a cast was not much of an issue at home. Our townhouse is two-story. I would get up and down the stairs by sitting on each step, lifting myself with my arms and pushing off the good leg. And when I got to the landing, I would use my good leg and push myself up. Got to love my ballet and dancing for the strength I had in my core and my legs.

When the cast came off, my leg was weak and thinner. I noticed it and i ignored it. That was normal, was it not. I mean the foot and leg had been in a cast and the muscles were inactive. Right? Maybe not.

Three months later, although he was weak and frail, my father was cleared to go home - only to be re-hospitalized 48 hours later. There was blood in his stool. The doctors suspected a bleeding ulcer and so they scoped. And they scoped. They found nothing. Within a few days though, a red bump (growth) appeared by dad's sternum. And it kept growing. The doctors were perplexed. They assumed it was being caused by an infection. So exploratory surgery was scheduled.

The doctor who did this investigative operation was very happy to tell my mother and me that it was not an infection. Whereas my mother was relieved at the so-called good news, I looked straight at him and asked, "if it isn't an infection, then what is it?" He did not know, and there was '*nothing more they could do for him*'. And so, a few days later they sent him home, again.

It is strongly suggested that people with MS meditate and remain stress free. Clearly, this was not happening in my case.

I think dad knew that was the last time he was going to see his house, his car, his garden. He looked at everything slowly and deliberately. As if he wanted to memorize everything. He was not home more than 12 hours. That very night he was rushed back to the hospital, dad was feeling worse. At the hospital we were told he was bleeding internally. They started irrigating his heart. I was by his side the following evening, in the isolation ward.

Three days later, at my visit with dad, I noticed that his beautiful brown eyes were, what I can only describe as cloudy. And when I looked at the irrigating system, I noticed the water was bloody. It should have been clear. I did not say anything because I did not want to alarm him. It was Saturday evening, the last Saturday of dad's life.

We talked for a while, he was not in any pain and he was quite talkative. Suddenly one of the machines to which he was hooked up started to beep. He looked at it and said, "what now". As I replied that I would call a nurse, he took what was - his last breath. I was there. I saw him gasp; I saw what I assume looked like, his soul leaving his body.

And since it was Saturday evening, there were few doctors in the hospital, let alone specialists. The cardiologist on call was summoned. Before she got there, two bags of blood were pumped into dad. The nurses were preparing the third bag of blood as the cardiologist arrived. I saw her talking with the nurses. I wanted to yell at her to cut the chit chat and take my dad to the operating room and fix him. Do it now!

Finally, after what seemed like an eternity, dad was taken to surgery (good God, another one). I called home. I told my husband to get a sitter and then to go get my mother and come to the hospital. I did not give any details. The eternal optimist in me was waiting for good news. I was wrong. *I was wrong.* The doctor could not help him. She could not fix him. He was pronounced dead on the operating table. And for years (and years), I harboured extreme guilt. I felt I could have saved his life had I summoned the nurse the moment I saw blood in the water.

I was defiant - to say the least. I would not leave the hospital until I could see my father, to say goodbye. The nurse allowed me to see him, but I was not allowed to touch him. I suspect under the covers; his chest was still open.

It is not true that a dead person looks like they are just sleeping. This man was my dad, but something was missing.

I requested an autopsy. The results indicated that the aorta had come apart at the sutures. The surgeon's voice rang in my ears. *"Had I known there was that much calcification, I wouldn't have agreed to do the operation."* I then also knew where the blood on his sternum was coming from. My poor dad. All that suffering. And yet his story did not end there. At the cemetery, he was buried at the wrong plot. *Wait, What!?!*

After dad's death I had to deal with the funeral arrangements. I was still walking and driving. The MS was still at the early stages. I went to the funeral home with my mother, to select a coffin, and to make the necessary arrangements for what was to be my father's final resting place. For his burial spot, my mother purposely selected a spot by a willow tree. He had always loved sitting under the shade of a tree. But somehow the funeral home got it wrong (screwed up). That is not where they buried him. At the service, in our grief neither, neither one of us had noticed. It was my brother-in-law who brought it to my attention later that day. My mother wanted him moved. I called the funeral home and arranged to have my father laid to rest in the 'correct' place.

I was at the funeral home/cemetery for the second burial. And I discovered my father's coffin had been changed. When I asked why the coffin was changed, I was told by the funeral director that the original coffin got damaged by the bulldozer used when dad was being exhumed, so they 'upgraded' and laid him in a better (more expensive) coffin.

Before the second interring, I asked the funeral director to open the coffin. My mother wanted me to verify that it was in fact my dad who lay inside, and *she* did not want to look. I agreed, I would give me a chance to say goodbye (again). The funeral director hesitated, and reluctantly complied.

WTH!!!

I felt like I had been doused with ice water. The inside of the coffin was raw wood. The lumberyard markings were visible. And my dad was wrapped in a shroud that had lipstick stains on it. I looked up at the funeral director. Calmly and in a low voice, said "I am too angry to even speak to you right now, but you will hear from me, t-o-d-a-y." I have no idea how I did it, but I remained eerily composed. I did not want my mother to suspect that anything was wrong. I saw no need to upset her.

After the coffin was lowered, we left. I drove my mother home and watched her enter her house. Then I drove down the street, and out of her viewing range. I pulled the car over. I called the funeral director and demanded an explanation. He told me my father's body had been placed in the coffin they used for people who had a viewing but who were later cremated. I told him I did not give a flying *bleep*, nor did I care to hear any more *bleeping* excuses. I told him he had until 2 o'clock that day to put my father in a coffin like the one we had originally selected, one that had cushions and silk inside. AND the funeral home was to credit my mother the cost of the original coffin she had bought. I was livid. I did not give him a chance to reply. I slammed shut my mobile. At 2 o'clock I was at the cemetery again. To bury my father - a third time.

Oddly enough, the following year, that same funeral home purchased one of my paintings at an auction at which I was displaying my work. It was not the same the same director who made the purchase.

CHAPTER 7

Knock Knock. MS re-calling, no denying.

A week after dad's death, I went back to work. I was walking in the office, and I tripped, over the carpet. Seriously?! And a few days after that, I developed a huge uneasiness in my sciatic nerve. As hard as I tried to ignore it, the uneasiness grew until even I had to admit I was in pain. At home and in the office, I could get up and walk about. But sitting in the car was excruciating. I was shifting in the seat every 40 seconds. It was awful. Extremely uncomfortable and equally embarrassing.

I was in pain, and I could not get relief. Sitting was bothersome, standing was frustrating, lying in bed was so difficult. I could not find relief. Walking was somewhat tolerable. For someone who hated taking pills, I was popping ibuprofen – 5 pills at a time. After a few sleepless nights I decided to go to the ER.

I was examined by two separate doctors. They poked my feet with needles; instead of feeling obvious discomfort, I felt they were tickling me. The doctors checked my reflexes and made me move various ways. They agreed on their diagnosis. I was suffering from nothing more than 'tension in my muscles'. So, I was prescribed muscle relaxants and told that the pills would probably knock me out, and not to be surprised if I felt like sleeping all the time. That weekend my family and I were driving to Toronto to visit my sister. The only good thing those pills did was to allow me to sit for the 5-hour car ride without shifting and tossing. Not once did I feel sleepy. By the end of the weekend, the muscle relaxants were useless.

About the same time, my thyroid started going crazy.
Hypo one week, hyper the next. Coincidence? Maybe.

Within weeks, the symptoms flared even more. I was tripping and falling over a blade of grass, a speck of dust, in other words over everything and nothing. I had to deliberately think of every step I took. I was still wearing high heels, but my left leg was dragging. My gait was obvious, and people were starting to notice and to ask me what was wrong. In addition, I was losing my balance, enough that I was afraid to walk alone. I recall one Saturday morning visit to the farmer's market. I was losing my balance so much that I was afraid to walk between aisles, afraid that I would topple over into the stands. My balance was that bad. I told myself it was time to get flats, shoes without heels. I told myself that would help me walk straight.

My mother had a doctor's appointment coming up. I tagged along and spoke to the doctor. He was uneasy with what I was describing, with what I was feeling and experiencing. And I didn't like the concerned look on his face. He gave me a referral to see a neurologist. It was the same neurologist to whom my OBGYN had sent me to 10 years earlier.

I got an appointment. Since my condition wasn't considered an emergency, the appointment was scheduled four months later. In the meantime, I was in pain, so I sought and found another neurologist. I went to see him. He listened to everything I told him. Then he hooked about 20 needles to different parts of my leg and hooked the other ends up to some machine. And even though I was told it would hurt, I felt nothing.

> *I did not like this doctor. He was more interested in selling me new needles, (stating the old ones would hurt because they were not as sharp as a new set). I do not know what he found, but I never went back to him. I did not like his interest in money more than his interest in healing.*

Patiently, and with no other choice, I waited out the four months to see the neurologist my GP had recommended. Fortunately, after a month and a half, the sciatic nerve had stopped bothering me. And I had stopped tripping over things that were not there. I was exercising. Strengthening my leg and stretching my sciatic nerve. When I finally saw the (recommended) neurologist, I told him everything. Including the fact that I thought I had MS. (A feeling I got right at the first fall in the park, months before). He examined me, my reflexes, my strengths, my flexibility my reaction time. He pushed and pulled and tapped. He asked if I had any changes in my vision or if I needed to urinate more often. The answer was no to both.

Hmm. I remember thinking that maybe it was not MS. I wasn't experiencing any of what he was asking. Dr. C. scheduled me for an MRI. Normal wait times for scheduled MRIs are long. My neurologist thought the delay would be close to eight months. But I got scheduled to have my MRI done three months later. That was amazing. In the meantime, although I was not tripping anymore, my left leg had become significantly weaker.

I used to play pitch and catch with my son, to help him practice his baseball. Although we had been doing this for a while, suddenly I could no longer run for the ball. My left leg was dragging. I could not run. And I was not walking at my regular pace either. My gait was worse. But I could cope, and I could cover. I excused these 'indicators' by telling people that my walking cast came off not too long ago and my leg was still weak. They believed me. Why would they not. They had no reason to doubt me. Then slowly, the strength in my left arm became feeble. I needed both hands to hold a full pot of coffee.

What I could not control though, and couldn't cover up, was my loss of balance. I could not walk without losing my balance. It was as if I was drunk. I did not dare go up or down a set of stairs without holding on to the banister for dear life. And if I was somewhere where there were steps without a banister, I needed to hold onto someone. I was still grieving the loss of my father, and now I had looming over me the possibility of MS. I was dropping weight. I did not mind that, (what woman does). But the grief and worry were showing on my face.

The loss of balance stopped. Well (actually or maybe) not on its own. I went to see a healer. I did not understand what he did, I still don't, but what he did, helped. He explained to me that he had a gift, he could see my cells. And the ones he saw as blue were damaged. He changed them back to their normal state of white. He worked on both ears and that was that! I still do not fully understand how, but what he did, worked. I was so relieved. I did not walk like I was drunk anymore.

I had my MRI. Months passed, and nobody had called me with the results. Neither from my neurologist's office nor from the hospital where the MRI was done. I did not want to know the results, but I knew I had to. Reluctantly I called and made an appointment to be given my results. It cost me $20 in parking to learn what I did not want to know.

I was informed that there were lesions on my brain, similar with what is present in patients who have Multiple Sclerosis. *Argh.* Similar with; maybe they were wrong. I did not want to contact my neurologist. I did not want to get confirmation.

I was in shock. And in disbelief. I do not know if I was in actual denial, but I was in disbelief. I left the hospital where I was just given my results and drove straight to a bookstore. I looked for every book on Multiple Sclerosis and started reading. Myleene sheathe, auto-immune, lesions, life expectancy, hereditary, North America, Beta Ferron, diet, neurologist, wheelchairs, MS and pregnancy, assistance.... **STOP!!** I did not want to know what it was; I did not want to know the symptoms nor what to expect; I wanted to know how to treat it, how to stop it. Which book has those answers?! Which one!!!

I went home. Or did I go pick up my son at daycare. I do not remember. I knew for certain that was I was not going to tell anyone. I was going to fight this. I was going to defeat this disease, this monster. No one need know. I was going to beat this and then teach others how to stomp it. I thought of the people I knew who struggled with MS. How old were they when they got it? How old are they now? How fast did they go downhill? One of the books gave a life expectancy. I calculated how old I would be and how old my son would be .... Stop! I was determined to beat this. Welcome denial 😳.

My mind took a turn.

I love shoes. I love high heels, I love funky shoes, I love sexy shoes ... I love shoes. And I had an extraordinary array of shoes, expensive shoes which I had bought at sales, at reduced prices. And since I was so good on shoes, they lasted me forever. I won't say I had a lot of shoes and boots, but I did. And I loved it! Damn it! Having MS would change everything.

In my mind I started cataloguing which shoes I would be able to wear, which heels I would still be able to rock without falling, and which I would have to give up. For now. Because I was going to beat MS and get back to wearing all my gorgeous shoes. After all, I had done it before. I had edema during my last trimester of pregnancy, and I could not wear my shoes. But two weeks after giving birth the shoes were back on my feet. I did it then. I was going to do it again.

Funny isn't it. I had received life altering news and I was fixated on my ability to wear my shoes. Huge denial!

I could not be sick. I was feeling fine. Ok, so my leg was a little weak, and I was walking slower, but I felt fine. I felt fine. There was nothing wrong with me. I was fine! Was anyone listening? God, can you hear me? I'M FINE. In my mind, this was all a mistake. It was all nothing more than a misdiagnosis. I WAS FINE!

I told my husband what happened at the hospital, the results of the MRI. But in doing so, I downplayed it. A couple of lesions, just a couple. It could be Multiple Sclerosis, but they aren't sure. I lied and added that it could be a weakness from the cast. Others were buying that excuse, maybe he would too. I knew he would not look anything up. I knew he would have his suspicions, but he would not investigate. I also told him that I did not want anyone to know anything. My mother knew I had gone for an MRI but she hadn't asked whether or not I had received the results. No need to tell her anything. It was strange though, that she had forgotten. She was usually on top of everything. I assumed since she was still grieving my father's death, this slipped her mind.

I didn't realize this was possibly her calling card from the dementia, which was making in her, its new home.

George respected my request not to tell anyone. But he watched me. He watched my every move. And so, I walked ever so carefully, I did not want any anomaly to show. There was a wee (huge) problem with that though. It was not easy to turn off everything in my mind and think only of the steps I was taking. It was like trying to think of each breath breathed, or each heartbeat, or each blink. Who can do that?! I am a master multitasker. Always have been. I can walk and chew gum at the same time 😊, but this was so difficult, I would say even impossible.

It was so difficult to turn off my brain to everything else, and to think only about walking. My first *oopsie* happened in the house. I was coming down the stairs, and I went ass over teakettle. Fortunately, the stairs and floor were carpeted. And just as fortunately I missed hitting the walls and furniture. Even though I did not break any bones, falling down the stairs does leave bruises. Furthermore, falling down the stairs, and tripping over specs of dust were not acceptable occurrences.

I knew the results of my MRI, certainly my neurologist must have received them. Yet nobody from his office had called me to book a follow-up consultation. And so, I called. I called and got an appointment for a (follow-up) appointment, I had to do some serious maneuvering to do. I had to get my ducks in a row.

- My GP was also my mother's GP.
- She was present when he gave me the referral to the neurologist.
- If the neurologist has the results of the MRI he would have surely shared them with the referring doctor who might inadvertently tell my mother or ask her a question.

I did not want my mother to be aware of anything. She was dealing with the loss of my father, and she saw me as her lifeline. I did not want her to know that I (may) have Multiple Sclerosis. She would not have been able to handle it. And I certainly did not want to handle her not handling it. I notified my GP's office, not to answer any questions my mother may have had regarding me.

Fast forward a couple of months. I went to my neurologist's office. I did not want to spend another $20 for parking so I circled the nearby streets (over and over), until I found a spot, where two-hour parking was allowed. Plenty of time I thought to myself. But being a specialist with many patients, Dr. C. was late. And since there was a patient waiting ahead of me, I kept a close eye on my watch. (A psychologist would have had a field day with what I was thinking and how I was dealing). My turn came. Dr. C. was very sympathetic when he confirmed the diagnosis of MS, and almost apologetic when he told me that although there was no known cure, there were medications to ease the pain and delay the progression. (I have to say, Dr. C. is a doctor with fantastic bedside manner!)

No thank you. I did not want steroids with their horrific side effects on the off chance that they 'may' ease the severity by 30%. I am not a gambler. And I was not going to start by taking odds with my life on steroids. I told him so. Dr. C. said he wanted to see me again in 3 months.

I was angry. Not at him, at everything! As I was waiting for the receptionist to book my next appointment, I mumbled under my breath (at least I thought it was under my breath), something about the doctor being late and that I hoped not to have a parking violation. Dr. C. heard me and moved close to me. He told me if I had received a parking ticket, to bring it to him. He would pay it. Of course, I would never do that, but his caring, his empathy and his compassion touched me.

I left Dr. C.'s office and went straight to work. I was more productive than normal. I concentrated only on work. I immersed myself on the jobs and projects sitting on my desk. And I must have been emitting a 'stay away' vibe because people did in fact stay away. *Yikes.*

When I got home, I told my husband all that happened, all about the visit with the doctor. Again, I told him I did not want anything said to anyone! My mother seemed to be accepting the answers I was giving her, that my leg was weakened by the walking cast. But I was afraid that she and my sister (in Toronto) would talk, and that my sister would connect the dots for her. I realized I had a loose end which required immediate attention. So, I called my sister and told her what was happening, and I asked, begged her, NOT to tell anyone anything.

There is a Greek expression I learned from my mother, one she used often enough; *'you cannot hide love, you can't hide a cough, and you can't hide deception'*. Not quite a month later, I found out that my sister had disclosed the secret she had vowed to uphold. Whatever her reasons, she betrayed me and my trust in her. She did not keep her word. I confronted her and told her I was hurt, frustrated and disappointed with her actions. She did not deny any of it. And to her credit, she did not come up with any lame excuses. She knew and understood I was hurt. I am glad she understood. Because that became the last time, I put her in a similar situation. And it has been 20 years.

There are 2 things I hate. They are both being lied to.

The 3 months leading to my next appointment went well. I had no visible changes. Unfortunately, neither did I have any improvements. I had also started looking for and trying any type of alternate healing available. I adamantly knew, I did not want to take the steroids route.

The first thing I tried was meditation. Argh. Quieting my mind for 5-15 minutes every morning was hell not easy. I remember driving out to nature parks to be around peace and tranquility. I was told to hug a tree. Um – no! That is NOT me. I am not in any sense of the term, a tree hugger. I do not even leave the bathroom in the morning without putting mascara on. But I did give meditation a try, albeit half-assed. That was my first attempt at alternative healing.

At my next appointment with the neurologist, I told him that I would continue seeing him if, and only if, he promised not to tell me what type of MS I had, how I was doing, or anything about the disease – unless of course it was that a cure has been found. I was determined to get better and I did not want my brain to register anything to the contrary. He reluctantly agreed. But he had a strategy. He had his nurse talk to me about a new treatment. It involved injecting myself every other day with some poison that had certain *possible* side effects. But - the medication did come with a video depicting other MS patients tiptoeing through the tulips - thanks to this drug. All for only $1,300 a month!

Against my better judgment, I agreed to try it. I learned how to prepare the syringe and how to inject myself. I had to do so because there was absolutely no way my husband would inject me; it simply wasn't going to happen. He would have passed out. As it was, just knowing I was injecting myself every other day gave him palpitations and made him sweat from every possible orifice. Poor guy tried to hide it and stand strong. He tried anyway. 😄

And so (I reiterate), against my better judgment, I used this drug for 4 months. I did not suffer any of the reported side effects, so I know my body was not rejecting any of its weird and wacky (supposedly wonderful) ingredients. What it did though, even though the neurologist could not explain or justify it, was make me worse. This time I listened to my instincts, I listened to my body. Goodbye to the poisoning crap with which I was injecting myself.

I am a positive person. The positive I took from that whole experience, is I learned how to give a painless injection.

At one follow up visit, as I was leaving the neurologist's office, a woman followed me into the hallway, stopped me and excused herself for taking liberty and for the interference. She told me about a healer in Chinatown who did amazing work with acupressure. Acupressure? I had heard of and was familiar with acupuncture, but I did not know what acupressure was; other than what the term insinuated. I decided to try this alternative healing too. After all, this had to be a sign. Seriously, what were the odds of getting approached by a total stranger, at the end of a visit with the neurologist, and get told of a healing method that was helping her and a friend of hers. I did not ask for any of her personal details. I just made note of the acupressurist name and location. I went home, looked him up and made an appointment.

If anyone out there reading about this, who has ever been to an acupressurist, they know exactly what followed. Thanks to the MS, every nerve in my body was set to super sensitive. Every touch, poke, rub etc. felt 100 times more intense. As I stated earlier, my pain tolerance threshold is considered very high. Well! Either this threshold was destroyed by the disease, or this acupressurist would have put a normal person into a coma. This small man did not use his hands alone. He had a drawer full of torture tools. At one point I thought he was Attila, reincarnated.

I thought for sure that my shrills would have scared off people sitting in the waiting area, or that anyone hearing them would have called the police. But no. And believe it or not, I truly felt better after every 20-minute session. It would have been worth my pains, screeching and hollering (not to mention taking 2 hours from work every week) if the results lasted for more than a few hours. Although I had much more strength and mobility leaving the cave of torture, the next morning my body would return to its limp immobile state.

I am not a quitter. Pain or no pain, I was determined to follow through with the suggested twenty visits. So, I did. The positive taken away from those sessions was twofold. Firstly, I better understood how effective torture tactics were. This small framed 5 foot nothing, 100-pound 60 plus year old man could take down Goliath – and without a sling shot. Secondly, I learned that my muscles, tendons, nerves, and anything else under my skin was alive! My limbs were not only feeling pain, but they were involuntarily (or voluntarily) moving away from the source of it. This was good!

Another strikeout, another failed attempt at natural healing. And if acupressure did not work, maybe acupuncture would. I started my hunt for an acupuncturist willing to work with or on someone who suffered with MS. I found one. His office was at the other end of town. Not to miss too much work, I booked 7 a.m. appointments. I could get across town before traffic hour started and get to work only one hour late. (I stayed at the end of my normal day and made up the time). George took GM to school on the days I headed to these treatments.

Acupuncture was not painful. It felt tingly, and sometimes I would start bleeding a bit at the punctured spot, but I could not say I was in any pain or discomfort. And I felt good. For a year. The sessions helped me, but the results were short lived. I was walking (albeit gingerly), without a cane. And I was still able to drive. But to feel good, I had to see the acupuncturist twice a week.

The rest of the healings were a jumbled mess. I remember going to deep tissue massage sessions. And although I dealt with the pain and uneasiness, hiding the resulting bruises had not been easy. I looked like I was battered. I remember doing tap therapy. And touch healing and DNA history cleaning and visited at least six different osteopaths.

As if these attempts weren't enough, I continued my alternative healing with light therapy and motivational rituals and a truck load of special diets and expensive supplements. And then I found something new to try; one more thing. I found a healer who worked on the hot and cold zones in the body. After a few months, I stopped wasting his time and mine. Over the years of trying this and that, I had spent the equivalent of what could easily have been family vacations – for five years! All I lost, was the equivalent cost of five years family vacations.

Still, I refused to accept what the medical society and other professionals were saying. My mind kept telling me that there was a cure. And I was going to be proof of that. The human body instinctively heals itself. I needed to help it heal and to prove it to the world.

My body and my mind are stubborn. My body would not heal, and my mind would not accept that.

CHAPTER 8

My pregnancy

When I was a teenager, and in my early 20s, marriage and or children were not part of my plans. I wanted neither the responsibility nor the commitment. Especially not the responsibility; I had been responsible for someone or something ever since I could remember. I wanted to take time for me.

But by the age of 28 all I could think of was having a child. To have an extension of me. Someone I could love and bring up giving him/ her love and allowing him/her to be happy, more importantly to allow them to be a child. Something I had not experienced. I started reading books on child rearing, talked with friends who were already parents, and I spent a lot of time with their kids. I was looking at children's clothing, footwear, at children's books etc. I was getting ready. But I did not want a husband. I saw firsthand what crappy marriages were like, both from my parents and from my own first marriage.

That is when George re-entered my life. We discussed various things. We agreed; we were both ready to become parents. But it was not happening. I was not getting pregnant. I went to a fertility specialist.

All he did was help me lose my confidence. I was losing hope and I was getting angry. One day my mom suggested I visit a specialist she had heard of.

Normally I would have rolled my eyes and walked away. Another piece of advice she got from one of her know-it-all meddling friends who gave useless advice. But this time I listened. I took note of the doctor's name, made an appointment. The rest is a success story.
Thank you, Dr. T.,

The first part of my maternity was wonderful. And from my first ultrasound I was bonding with my wonderful son. I would talk to him, read to him, play music to him and dance with him. (And obviously he was happy being where he was. It took 48 hours of getting induced, and an emergency c-section for GeorgeMichael to make an appearance).

I was at the prime of my life. I was 32 years old, had a great job and I was 5 months pregnant. I could still wear cute clothes and rock high heels. My maternity was a good one. No morning sickness, no aches, no pains. I was walking and dancing and sleeping and was enjoying every day. Then, at month 6, my body decided to do a 180 (or is it a 360? I don't know which expression is accurate.) What I do know is I started swelling in weird places.

I had edema. From the waist up I was completely normal. I was my normal self. From the waist down however, I turned into The Michelin Man. My legs were one size from my thighs to my toes. There was no definition at the knee, or calf, or ankle. Yuk. Waking up in the morning, before even putting my feet on the floor, I had to put on shoes. Because if I didn't, my normal size 6 feet needed a size 8 1/2 slipper.

Fortunately, my 3rd trimester was during the summer months, I did not need boots or a coat. On the flip side though, I could not wear shorts or a skirt. There was no way I was going to show my legs. Although I felt fine, I looked like a fat clown. You know the kind that has a hoop around the middle.

Two weeks before my due date, I was at a Greek wedding. I danced all night. And I do not mean shuffling my feet to some slow music, I mean hopping and jumping to Greek folk dances. The guests at the reception were making wagers on what time that evening I would go into labour. But I didn't.

My due date came and went, but the baby did not. I was scheduled to be induced. My pregnancy term was up, and the baby was nowhere near the birthing canal. I was scheduled to be at the hospital on the upcoming Monday morning. I worked until the Friday before. Why would I stop earlier? I felt fine, and I wanted to have as much of my 15-week maternity leave with my baby. (Yes, it was only 15 weeks back then.)

I was induced for a day and a half. I had a monitor strapped on me to follow my heart rate and that of the fetus. The monitor indicated contractions, but I felt nothing. No labour pains at all! The nurse told me I was lucky. She told me I was 1 in about 8,000 women who did not feel contractions. Halfway through the second day (of being induced), the doctors decided to intentionally break my water and help the little guy make a move. But when they examined me, they realized they shouldn't / couldn't. I was still carrying much too high.

So high that I could not even have a normal c-section. I had to have what they referred to as an emergency c-section. I was cut open where my belly was extended the most.

My sweet baby boy was well worth every delay; worth every test and medication I was given. Within three weeks, my little sweetheart was completing 12-hour nights. His pediatrician told me I was very fortunate. He even suggested I not tell anyone because they would resent my good fortune. Additionally, I never once had to change a crib at 3:00 in the morning. I did not have to deal with teething issues or earaches. Of course, he had illnesses and childhood scares. But he was the type of child who made parents more than happy to have more. And we tried. But it was not to be. I had 3 miscarriages after successfully having GM.

I vividly remember my first miscarriage, because of the guilt I felt. When I found out I was pregnant again, I was overjoyed. That same night, as I finished singing GM a lullaby, before I put him in his crib, I wondered if and how I could possibly love another baby the way I loved him. I miscarried, the very next day. I carried that guilt for a very long time.

CHAPTER 9

Time to tell my son of my condition

I had been to the neurologist. I had sought out all alternative treatments I could find. I had exercised as much as possible. And I kept my condition a secret. My husband knew as did my sister (and her friends). I walked cautiously, I excused any trips or missteps and blamed the break and cast for as much as possible. But I was tripping more and more. One day, my little guy teasingly said," mom, you're getting to be a spaz". It was time to tell him.

GM was 10 years old. I drove us to a coffee shop. I picked up a tea for me and a shake for him and we went down to the Lakeshore, the waterfront. We used to go to the Lakeshore before school some mornings and feed the ducks. It was our chill place. And our place to discuss issues and events. I told him about my condition. I was careful not to let any emotions show. I stated only the facts, and at that, only the bare minimum. I told him that I would answer honestly any questions he had. He did not have any, but he wanted to be able to ask me later, as questions came up.

GM has always been close to me. Very close. Almost like my protector. While I was carrying him, I could feel him moving inside me and I would instinctively put my hand on my belly. If anyone else (including his father) put their hand on me to feel his movements, he would give them what I imagine was a kick to get away. It was hysterical. And when he was about 2 years old, if his dad tried to get close to me, GM would push him away and with a very serious tone and look, would tell him "No hugging, no kissing".

I was concerned at the fact that he did not have any questions, I didn't want him to bottle anything up. But true to who he is, he looked up everything about the disease. He knew what was happening to me, what to watch for, how to help me. And help he did, with a twist of humour. Never (to this day) have I ever felt handicapped when with him.

I continued doing everything I did before. I took GM to his baseball games and practices. I took him to his tennis lessons. I took him to soccer. I was the escort mom on school field trips. I recall taking GM and his friend Stuart to LaRonde (an amusement park here in Quebec). We spent the day there. I sat every chance I got. I could not get involved in any of their fun, but I made sure not to impede on it either.

Of course, as the years progressed my mobility deteriorated, and I needed a cane. I was more concerned about GM than I was about me. I asked him if my need for the cane embarrassed him. The mothers of all his friends were normal. He looked at me and made a grimace. I understood. He did not have a problem. To him I had not changed. I was still me.

I am so grateful that I was healthy during his younger years, the years we hung out. We had fun. We did so much together. And until GM got married, we had our mother / son night - once a month or so. We went out, had dinner together and discussed everything under the sun. He still takes me out. If not to one of his ball games, then shopping. And I've got to love Kate, my beautiful daughter-in-law. She looks out for me too.

PART FOUR ...

"A beautiful face will age, and a perfect body will change.
But a beautiful soul will always be a beautiful soul."
..... Rakesh Mishra

CHAPTER 10

My Angels

GM now knew what was happening, what I was living. It was time to tell the angels in my life, my friends. Haydeh first. Haydeh and I have been neighbours for 31 years, friends for 30 and inseparable friends for 29. She is amazing. As far as I am concerned, everyone should have a friend like Haydeh in their life. She has been with me through so much. Every step of everything, good and bad. Like marriage vows, for richer or poorer, in sickness and in health. When I needed to share happiness, she has been there. When I had sorrow, I could turn to her. She was there when I needed a shoulder, when I needed to hide something, ask advice, or if I simply needed her presence, she has always been there.

Haydeh is petite but that never stopped her from loading and unloading the wheelchair from the trunk of her car, from folding and bending my legs when they refused to budge, and from pushing the wheelchair up hills and over rough terrain. Whenever I wanted to go somewhere, she made herself available - and smiled. She never hemmed or hawed. To this day, if I am not grocery shopping with her, she will buy for me things she knows I like. (Dave, her husband makes awesome bread. And when he does, he brings me a loaf.)

Angel number two is Johanne (at work). From the day I started working with her, she has been by my side. Figuratively and literally. One day we were going to a luncheon for a colleague. While we were being served our soup, I leaned over and whispered in her ear that I had MS. The shock on her face was huge. I asked her to keep my secret and she did. She watched out for me - incessantly. While I was using my cane or walker, she was right next to me.

Jojo (Johanne) bought me my first cane. She watched me struggle with my mobility and knew me well enough, she knew I would fight needing assistance and I would not give in and admit I needed one.

And when I transitioned into a wheelchair, she was there for all my transfers, and she wheeled me everywhere. When we had luncheons at work, she would serve me before she would serve herself. Johanne would gift me with musicals and plays and shows, knowing so well how much I enjoyed those outings. And she still makes sure I get as much pleasure during our outings - as much as possible.

It was time, I had to finally tell my other friends of my condition. And although they had figured it out, they respected my silence. Mary is my oldest friend. We have known each other since we were in grade school, and we have gotten into mischief together for decades. Mary is very busy, but she always makes time to spend with me. She brings me things from her garden or servings of meals she made. Every holiday both Mary and her mom bring me home made delicacies.

And although I don't see her as often Esther and her mom visit and bring me home made yummies. Our visits are never long enough. I have been friends with Esther for a little over 20 years. Same goes for Elizabeth, whom I've known since I was 16. Liz is also godmother to my son. Elizabeth and I can go months without touching base, and when we do connect it's as if we had spoken the day before. My friends who live out of town are equally precious to me. Thanks to technology, we are always in touch.

People who have met me since the wheelchair have accepted me straight out. Even without knowing the 'normal' me, they like who I am now. Funny story, one Christmas we were at Cindy and John's. (Cindy and John are the wonderful parents of my beautiful daughter-in-law). I leaned up against a chair and stood up so I could put on my coat. I heard Cindy say that until that moment, she did not know how tall I was.

Do I miss normal interactions? You bet I do. While my friends accept me for who I am now, I miss being who I was. I miss my sexy shoes. I miss being active. I miss my independence and I MISS DANCING.

PART FIVE ...

"Cages aren't made of iron.
They are made of thoughts."
….. Madhuri Khatri

CHAPTER 11

MEMORIES

In writing this book (aka therapy), many memories have crept up, and at oddest times. Good memories and not so good memories.

1.The sound of dad shaving.

I have two washrooms where I live. One of the bathrooms is quite large, with double sinks. It is often and perfectly normal that I would be in there brushing my teeth while George would be shaving. One day, inexplicably, one of my favourite memories surfaced.

When I was a little girl, in the first house I remember, I used to sit on the edge of the bathtub and watch my dad(dy) shave. I remember the pattern. He would squeeze the shaving cream (from a tube) onto his finger and dab the cream on his face. As I write this, I can visualize the light blue dots on his face and, I can smell the clean soapy scent. Then dad would wet his shaving brush and swirl it around his whiskers. The light blue dots turned into lather. (It amused me to watch him work the lather around his mustache.) He would either turn around and put some lather on the tip of my nose or make eye contact with me in the mirror (on the front of the vanity) and give me a wink.

Dad would then take his razor and twist the bottom which in turn opened the top portion, the part which housed and held the razor blade. He would carefully take the blade out of the folded waxy paper and he would slide it into the razor and close it in place. Then came my favourite part. The sound of the blade chopping off his whiskers.

It was a combination swishy - light scratching - scraping sound. I would be memorized, and I would not budge until that blade was removed from the razor, rinsed, and dried, returned to its wrapper, and tucked safely away in the vanity. Again, in writing this, I can hear the light squeak of the hinges on the vanity, and the click of the metal fastener. I do not know if magnet fasteners existed back then. It did not matter. Our vanity had a metal clasp. I remember that vanity, it was white with a little bit of rust here and there. And it was a slightly warped.

2. The little piano.

One year, Santa (aka mom) gifted me a little toy piano for Christmas. Money was tight; now that I think about it, mom must have done without something to afford it. It was a small little thing. I do not think it had more than 16 keys, if that many. And it had 3 little screw on feet, about 2 inches long. I also remember numbers printed on the keys. (How and why am I remembering these seemingly useless details?)

After dad screwed on the feet, he placed the toy piano on a flat surface, and with one finger he played Jingle Bells. The keys were so small that he had to be careful not to hit two at the same time (his fingers were obviously bigger than the tiny ones of a child, for whom this toy piano was intended). I was enchanted that dad played Jingle Bells. He hadn't any musical background.

I played with that piano daily. I would play until the cacophony got on my mom's nerves and she would take my piano away. But then one day something (remarkable) happened. I unintentionally hit the key marked #3, and I recognized the sound it made to be the first note to Jingle Bells, the tune dad had played days before. I remember the pause - while my brain registered the sound. And then it was like something was unlocked inside me.

I played Jingle Bells. Like I had heard dad play it days before. I played it again and again. I wanted to play more. I wanted to play something else. What? What? How? Both my parents loved music. Dad was always whistling a tune and mom was always singing. Then it came to me. I had heard mom singing 'Never On Sunday'. After some minutes of trial and error, I played the song, as much of it as I could on the 16 available keys.

My parents recognized I had a musical talent which could or should be developed. They started looking for a piano teacher. One with whom they could somehow barter and reach a fee arrangement. They could not afford lessons, let alone an actual piano. My dad gave up the search, but my mother did not. She wanted me (and my sister) to have some culture. And in her search for a music teacher, she found a ballet teacher. One she could afford. So much for getting me piano lessons; ballet lessons it was going to be.

Every time I saw a piano, I played it. Most of the times with only one hand; and after a few minutes of hunting and pecking, I played whatever tune I wanted. When I was in my teens my sister bought a guitar. I learned how to play 7 chords; 7 chords which allowed me to play folk songs and a good deal of Simon and Garfunkel tunes. Marina too learned to play the guitar, but her forte was in vocals. Could that girl sing!

When the Multiple Sclerosis took a solid hold on my body, Peggy, a woman I know, suggested that I relax by playing the piano. She had one in her house. When I visited her, I could not get enough time playing it. I bought an electric keyboard from the famous music store, Costco☺. I played, and I played, and I played that thing. I played at all hours, night, and day. I used to plug in headsets to keep from waking up the whole house.

I had no problem playing with one hand, and I was learning to play with two. But the effects of the disease increased, and so my keyboard time decreased. I could not control my fingers. Knowing it was in the house was a reminder of what I could not do anymore thanks to my unwanted parasite ☹. I reluctantly sold the keyboard.

3. Dancing with my parents.

Ever since I can remember, I loved dancing. Apparently, I moved a lot while my mother was pregnant with me. My mother used to say that she was either carrying a soccer player or a ballet dancer. My parents liked to dance, although they never danced with each other at home. At social gatherings however, it was a different story. They would tear up the dance floor. There was always music in our house. Even alone, someone was always dancing or singing.

Dad said that one Sunday we went to church earlier than our regular time. When the organist started playing, I got up on the pew, stretched my arms toward him and said "music, daddy dance". Of course, my sister and I did the patented stand on daddy's feet and dance with him. He would dance around with us often. And poor dad had corns. So, we had to watch where we stood.

I was 4 years old when I had mastered all the Greek folk dances; my mother had taught me all the dances she knew. There are photos and home movies of me folk dancing at wedding receptions. Yup. The little flower girl had musicality and did not miss a step. I loved to dance. I still do. Have I mentioned that? Maybe a few times, right ☺.

My mother (also) loved to dance, and she knew almost every dance style. She taught me to tango, to twist, to rock and to waltz. She taught me every ballroom style dancing she knew and every Greek folk dance she knew too. What she did not teach me, I learned by watching others. On weekends my parents either had friends over at our house, or we would be visiting their friends. Either way, there was always music and dancing involved. Without fail, furniture would be moved, and the dancing would start.

When I was old enough to go out dancing with my friends, my mother was all too happy to join in for an hour or so. Then she would leave. If I showed up without my mother, someone in the group would go get her.

Not only did I love to dance but I was good at it. I still have a very tarnished silver cup I won at a dance competition; it was for my waltz. When I studied ballet, I achieved/rated either second or third in my grade. Damn it, hard as I tried, I never attained first place.

I remember a certain ballet recital at which I was to perform. My mother had forgotten about it. It was a Sunday afternoon, and my parents were hosting some of their friends. I was 8 years old and as luck would have it, I was wearing a red dress my mother had made me. It had big ruffles at the end of the sleeves and on the skirt. And on the ruffles were beautiful ballerinas. The phone rang, it was my ballet teacher,

Mademoiselle Legris, looking for me. My dad rushed me to the recital, and I performed in my red ballerina dress.

4. Shopping, walking, and taking off.

My mother and I were shoppers (I still am). I think we knew every store in our city, and what it carried. We were as comfortable in a boutique as we were in a hardware store. Whenever my mother was not working, and I wasn't studying or whatever, we would be shopping or walking downtown. We enjoyed it. We rarely bought anything, but we had a blast. It was from her that I learned to make the most of a dollar. I am so grateful to her for that.

We went to shows, we went to restaurants, and we traveled a lot. Mom had friends in England, in Italy, in France, and in the USA (New Jersey, Florida and in California) … and she and I visited them all. (Dad was more of a home body).

Expo 67 happened in my lifetime and in my city. And we visited as a family. But my mother and I visited almost every day. I had so many stamps in my Expo passport, additional pages were required.

5. My sister moved out.

My mother was very strict. She was an authoritarian -- excessively strict. Is there a word stronger than excessive? She and my sister always butted heads. I did not like arguing. So, I just analyzed what I wanted to do, how badly I wanted it, what the consequences would have been, and whether or not the consequences (aka known as my mother's wrath) were worth facing. That was typically me.

My seemingly layback attitude was like my dad's. We seemed calm and cool, like we had it all under control. In reality though, we kept all the turmoil under wraps.

My sister and my mother were entirely different from me and my dad. When they had a thought or an idea, they would make it happen come hell or high water. And God help anyone who got in their way.

My mother's authoritarian rules were far too disproportionate, and my sister decided she had had enough. She decided she would free herself. She was going to move out. My mother sensed that something was brewing. And so, in her wisdom, (yes, wisdom is the adjective I am *sarcastically* selecting), she was going to prevent it (whatever *it* was) from happening. She highly suspected that my sister was getting ready to free herself. I believe my mom saw much of herself in my sister. Instinctively she knew what my sister would be thinking.

Mom was the last to leave the house in the morning, and the first one back in the afternoon. In her mind, she had it all under her control. She waited until each of us left the house to head to work or school. And to ensure we (specifically my sister) could not get back into the house, my mother would put the safety chain on the front door, and she would exit using the back door. There was only one key to the back door, and my mother had it.

No one knew of her *new* ritual. Until the day my sister came home early to take her things and found herself locked out. My sister kept her cool. When I got home, she told me about the chained door and then disclosed to me her altered plans. That night, before going to bed, she was going to unlock a basement window. The next day she would enter the house through that window, collect her stuff, and she would leave the same way. She had asked me if I was going to move out with her. I told her I would, but not by sneaking in through window. I was going to do it straight up, in and out the front door.

And true to her plan/word, my sister did exactly what she planned. That night, she unlocked a basement window, came back the next afternoon, collected her stuff, then left through the same window. I was not there when my mother came home from work, but I can only imagine her face when she saw the safety chain still on the front door, and all my sister's things gone.

> It is said, the more you 'police' someone, the more you teach them to become a better thief.

Today it is perfectly normal for kids to move away from home. But in a Greek household, especially in the 70s, there was no greater shame than to have a teenager, especially a daughter, move out.

When my dad came home from work, my mother told him that my sister was gone. AND, that it was MY fault because not only did I not stop her, but because I actually helped her. *Really mom. You dared blame me for all that happened.* My father looked like someone had just cut off his arms. He asked me if I was leaving too. I said yes. I was, I was going to pack and then say goodbye.

My father started to cry. I had only seen my father cry once before. I was 5 years old. My dad had received word that his father passed away. I remember dad walked to the living room, he sat on the end of the couch, and he cried. I went to him, I wanted to be with him. I did not know what to do, I just wanted to be with him so he wouldn't feel alone. He called to my mother to take me away. To this day I don't know if he wanted to be alone or if he didn't want me to see him vulnerable.

I had not seen him cry again, until that day. In a matter of 1 hour, he found out one daughter left (without a word), and he was about to lose another. I can still see his face and hear his voice as he asked me to stay. I was not expecting any of what had just happened. I had told my sister I would move and be with her. And my father, (the man I loved so much) was asking me to stay. I felt caught between the rock and hard place. Was I going to hurt my sister, or was I going to hurt my father. I felt frozen. I did not know what to do. It did not matter what I did, I was going to seriously hurt one of them.

I thought and thought. It felt like my stomach and my brain were going to explode. I had been my sister's keeper for 16 years, but my father's tears were killing me. I opted to calm my father. And in doing so, hurt my baby sister. I felt so mean, so nasty, so fickle. I had promised to share expenses with her. And I was not going to renege on that promise. She needed help, and financially at least I was going to be there for that, I would help her. I still remember her face too when I told her I was not moving in with her. I hated myself.

In the end, she didn't ask me for any financial assistance, she managed on her own.

PART SIX ...

"I will breathe.
I will think of solutions.
I will not let my worry control me.
I will not let my stress level break me.
I will simply breathe.
And I will be okay.
Because I don't quit.
..... Shayne McClendon

CHAPTER 12

21 years

It's been 21 years of trying. And whereas any sane person would have accepted their fate and given up, I still believe there is an answer, a cure out there. I will exhaust every possibility and perhaps even create options which are not yet there. I will be the person in her coffin thinking there is something else I should have tried. Or God willing, I will be one who beat the odds.

I smile a lot. I hope a lot. I love a lot. I laugh a lot. But I am also sad and dismayed. And even though I am surrounded by good people, I feel oh so lonely. My life has been a huge rollercoaster ride. I have had great highs, and I have had devastating lows. I grew up hearing stories of war and depression and perseverance and survival. I heard repeatedly how lucky my family was/is because things could be worse. Of course, that is true. But things could also be so much better. And while I do not want to be ungrateful, I will not be a pessimist. I choose to concentrate on the better. I want the better. I deserve and I am worth the better. And the better is what I want to leave my son and my grandbabies.

I totally expect to heal. I totally expect to help others. And I totally expect to do it in an affordable way. Searching for healing and help, is not cheap. And while I do not begrudge anyone for making a living, once I get healthy, I will pay it forward.

With every new therapy I have tried, any good results I experienced were short lived. Worse, when I lost whatever I had gained, for every step forward, it felt like I took two steps back. Almost as if my body was determined to punish me for trying to get better.

And for the last 5 years, my body has fallen under another attack shared by other members of the not so elite MS club. Swelling and inflammation. The swelling started mildly in my left arm. But the mild swelling got worse. My left arm is now 1" rounder than my right arm. Then my feet started swelling. Sometimes. Now they are swollen all the time. And it is not because my legs are hanging, neither is it because I am seated.

As did everybody else, I too thought the swelling was a result of being seated, of my legs hanging. So, I tried elevating them. For some reason, the swelling got worse. Possibly because by elevating my feet, I was putting pressure on the back of my legs. I saw a commercial for a foot massaging gizmo. The ad stated that all which was required, was to place my feet on this machine, and to set the switch to have the unit vibrate. The vibration would stimulate circulation in my legs, reduce pain, and reduce swelling. Whereas the vibration felt good, like a massage of sorts, that is all it did.

Not one to give up, I started elevating the bottom of my bed. I would stack a bunch of books under the mattress where my feet rested. The books did not stay put during the night. I decided to buy an electric bed base/frame so that I could tilt the bottom of the bed upwards. And I have been sleeping with my feet elevated for the last year-and-a-half. Unfortunately, I wake up in the morning with my feet just as swollen as they were the night before. Sometimes even worse. However, adjusting the bed makes sleep so much more comfortable.

I am by no stretch of the imagination, wealthy. But knock-on wood, I'm not starving. I have insurance, and I budget well. Which makes me wonder, what happens to people with a more limited income? What do they do when they arsh stricken with crappy diseases? Canes, walkers, wheelchair, support bars, modified washrooms, massage gizmos, therapies... these things are all expensive. Insurance (for those who have) pay a portion of it; I cannot help but wonder what happens to people with no insurance.

In Quebec (as I assume is the case in other provinces), we have buses modified to accommodate people who need assistance. And they are wonderful. But you must know at least 24 hours earlier that you will require the service. Unfortunately, that's not always how life works. Still, this service is a God-sent for people with mobility challenges, especially for people who need this service to get to and from work.

Back to the swelling. I am carrying an extra 30 plus pounds of swelling. I call is swelling because I do not know how else to describe it. It is not blood, it's not water, it's not fat. I have asked my neurologist what it could be, and he does not know. I have asked my GP what it could be, and he suggested I wear support hose. Which I tried. ☹ The swelling just moved to areas that the support hose did not cover. Argh. There are days that I look like the Michelin Man or the Pillsbury Doughboy. Actually, that's not true. You could see ankles on both the Michelin Man and the Pillsbury Doughboy. Whereas on me, there are no ankles.

I cannot wear boots; I cannot wear decent shoes. I can upsize my clothes, (reluctantly), but I cannot do the same with shoes and boots. My feet may be swollen but their length has not changed. Swollen or not, I am not a bigger size. And since I could still take some steps with the aid of my walker, and since I need to stand up to transfer, wearing shoes and boots that are too big make my very limited walking, pretty much more limited, and dangerous.

Let me recap all this. MS has robbed me use of my legs. My left arm is only 10%-20% functional. I cannot go anywhere where there are stairs. I cannot roll my wheelchair on grass or gravel or sand. I cannot go through a path that is not at least 28" wide. I cannot go to a restaurant or a mall or a park or a concert or to a friend's house, basically anywhere where there is not a washroom which has been adapted. I cannot wear anything cute; my clothes must be easy for me to get into. I cannot wear sexy shoes, I cannot wear skirts or dresses because of my swollen legs. Summer heat wears me down and putting on a warm winter coat requires some gymnastics. And going to the washroom - argh! - let's not get into that.

Sadly, and regrettably, many establishments think that by putting the wheelchair sign on their bathroom door, that they have suitably, adequately, and properly modified the facilities. Someone should tie their legs together and get them to attempt reaching the commode from a wheelchair, see if they can do it without falling on their face. It is sad, but there are very, very few establishments that are truly wheelchair friendly. Starting with the front door to their establishments. But that is another discussion for another time.

What most people take for granted are issues for me, some which require a good deal of planning. Take for instance going to the dentist. I must be sure to use the washroom before getting to his office. I need help to transfer from my wheelchair onto the dental chair. Helping someone who has MS, is not the same as helping an old person. An old person requires assistance. A person with MS, well, it is like dealing with unbalanced dead weight. Basically, you must make sure that we don't fall over and take you with us in the process.

Some MS sufferers have a certain amount of strength, but no balance. Others have even less. Unless the person who is helping has experience, we could fall and hurt us *and* you. Back to the example of going to the dentist. Should I need to use the facilities (Novocain will do that) the dentist has to stop what he is doing. I have to transfer back into my wheelchair, take the elevator down 3 floors because the only adapted washroom in the 6-story building happens to be on the floor where my dentist's office is not, then go back and transfer back into the dental chair. In the meantime, close to 10 minutes have elapsed.

A few years back, my son and his wife gifted me hair highlights (at the hair salon). Whereas I loved the results, I mean I absolutely loved them, the actual experience was horrible. I could not get from my wheelchair to the seat by the sink. It took 2 people to help make that happen. Then I had to get from the sink back into my wheelchair. It was traumatizing for me and for those who were trying to help. Going shopping, is just as hard. I cannot try anything on. I either have to go with someone who is my size (so that they can try things on for me), or I have to bring things home to try, and if I don't like how they fit, take them back.

Back in pre-MS days, I would get up at 5:00 in the morning. I would shower, then go downstairs and make myself a cup of tea. I would take an hour to myself, to read my book and drink my tea. Then I would head back upstairs to wake up my husband and my son, get myself ready for work, and get my son ready for school. Today, I still get up at 5:00 in the morning, but it takes me from the time I get up to 6:45 (the time I leave the house), to get washed, groomed, and dressed. And I need help. Often, I am by the sink brushing my teeth or putting on makeup when I realize I cannot rely on or utilize my walker. Either my knee is buckling, or my back won't hold me. So, I call out to my husband to bring me my wheelchair. To simplify things for me and for George, I now shower and wash my hair the night before.

I am grateful to be alive. I am not plugged into anything for survival. I have a bunch of people who love me. And I love myself. I think I love myself. Most of the time. Or sometimes. Honestly, I'm not sure of how I feel. Some days feel very dark Are these feelings of unsureness a result of my physical immobility, or are these pre-existing feelings, heightened due to my physical immobility. I do not know. I really don't. I do know however, that I fight feelings of depression, and deep feelings of loneliness.

> *"Be proud of who you are,*
> *and not ashamed of how others see you."*
> ..... *Amit Sodha*

The friends who know me from before my MS days tell me that they see me, not the wheelchair. They see me; not the physical person, but rather my zeal and love of life. New friends see the wheelchair. I do not know what I see when I look in the mirror. I am easy on the eyes. I am relatively intelligent, and I am a doer. And yet I feel confused. I recognize and acknowledge my accomplishments, but I do not know how I myself feel about the handicapped - sorry - the mobility challenged me.

I mentioned earlier that my life has been a series of ups and downs. No wonder I get dizzy easily ☺. Am I perpetuating the programs that belong to my ancestors? I see a lot of similarities in the lives lived by my grandmother and my mother. And how strange is it that both my sister and I have autoimmune illnesses. I mean how deep do DNA, genes and blood go. Could they determine the physical and para physical? If so, can I have a transfusion please.

So, what's next? Where do I go from here? What do I do next? Do I give up and accept what this disease has and is taking from me? Do I accept what is happening and find ways to adapt and make myself comfortable? Do I accept my loss of independence? Do I give in to being a burden? Nah. Not yet. Possibly not ever.

I work, albeit only 4 days a week. I love working. I see people, I talk with people. I get to use my brain and I am constantly learning. I'm productive and helpful. While everyone looks forward to a day off, I hate it. Even on the days when I do not go to work, I get up early, get dressed and groomed. I then get to into my motorized chair and zip zoom around my house. I read and I have either music playing or the TV on, for background noise. If Haydeh is home, we get together. If she is not available, I surf the net. And I do far too much online shopping.

Let me take you through a typical day. As I said, whereas I *used to* get up at 5:00 and get into the shower, I now shower and wash my hair before bed. This way, I get a few more minutes of sleep in the morning. The alarm on my mobile goes off. I use the mobile so I can choose and change what tune I use to start my day. I love music and I choose to start my day with a song, instead of an impersonal ring, chime, or techno notes. Then, I wake George. He helps me get out of bed. (I have a recliner in the bedroom. When I sleep on it, I do not need George's help.)

When I wake, before I stand up, I check my ankles and feet to see if they are swollen or if I can smile at normalcy. When they look good, I am ecstatic, like a kid on Christmas morning. On good days, I can use my walker to get to the washroom. When my legs decide not to work, I need my wheelchair, and lately, I have been using the wheelchair. After taking care of bio requirements, I head to the sink (where I stand). I brush my teeth and put on my makeup -- I mean – where I enhance my natural beauty. 😬

Then I shuffle or wheel back into the bedroom. I sit in my recliner and mentally plan for the day; has the garbage been taken out, do we need to make any stops for errands, what should be made for supper, and finally I mentally confirm that what I had planned to wear is still doable (weather wise). My husband is in the basement having tea, those are his words. What he is actually doing is having a cigarette. When he comes up, he helps me get dressed. Because my left arm does not work, I cannot snap hook or button anything. On with my earrings, necklace and or bracelet, and to the chair lift I go. We live in a split, the bedrooms are upstairs. I have a chair on a track that moves me up and down the stairs.

When I get downstairs, I transfer into my other wheelchair and get carted into the van. By this time, it's 6:45 a.m. George and I work at the same place. Convenient *n'est-ce pas*? George takes me to my desk where I transfer onto my office chair. Once I am settled, off he goes to his work area. I love working. I love the people with whom I work. I love the work I do. I will see George again before lunch if he has something of mine that required to be refrigerated, or to be reheated. If Johanne is at work, I take bio breaks when she does, and we have lunch together. If Jojo is not there, I eat by myself. When I see someone heading for the washroom, will also grab a ride with them (so to speak).

At 4:00 p.m. our workday is done. George comes and gets me, and we head home. Once home I will get in my wheelchair and while George prepares for supper, I take care of the mail, the bills, and anything else that requires attention. And in between taking care of the household, administrative and social requirements, I tell George what and how to prepare for supper.

Cooking is not George's forte. Except making rice. Everybody loves his rice.

I don't follow recipes; I know what foods will work well together. Plus, I use up what is in the fridge. I do not throw away food, even if it is only half a cup of leftovers. (I learned from my mother how to combine leftovers and present them as a new meal). George says I get this look on my face when the idea for a 'culinary concoction' hits me.

When supper is finished, George picks up and prepares lunches for the next day. He then takes a nap, waters the plants (summer), does a little gossiping with the neighbours, or goes downstairs to game with his online friends. I will take that time to read my email, talk with, text, or host a friend who has come for a visit. If the weather is good, I will sit out on the back deck and listen to my tunes. It is a routine - and I hate it. But I have no choice. I would so much prefer to go out for a walk (roll), but that does not happen. I will have a ramp installed by my front door even though my husband does not want one. He is not the one struggling to get out, I am. (He is afraid that in the winter, the ramp will be too icy to use).

At the end of the evening, it's back upstairs where I shower, wash my hair, and brush my teeth. George helps me get in and out of the shower. The step is high, and hard as I try, I can no longer clear it by myself. So, he grabs an ankle and moves my leg. When I finish, I roll into the bedroom, sit on the bed and George flips my legs on to it. The next morning the routine starts over. On days where I do not work but George does, I'm still downstairs by 6:45 a.m. Only this time my tea, my lunch and a snack are on the coffee table. So, I pretty much must know the day before how hungry or thirsty I will be. I could get into the kitchen but cannot do much when I'm in there. My kitchen is not modified. Reaching anything on the counter or in the fridge is pretty much impossible. Basically, everything is out of reach. Of course, the trickiest (and not so funny) occurrences on days when I am home alone, is when I drop something. If what is dropped cannot be retrieved, then it stays on the floor until George gets home from work. There have been times where Haydeh was home and has come to my rescue.

When Haydeh is available, we do things together. She will either take me to a mall, go to the Lakeshore, go for a drive/walk or just hang out and talk. She and I can talk for hours. And we both like going out. I remember the time she took me to St. Joseph's Oratory. Neither of us knew there was an area reserved for handicapped parking, so she parked in the general parking area, on the hill. Poor Haydeh pushed me uphill to the entrance. She got her exercise that day, and then some.

I am so lucky to have her. George and I are very different. George is a layback home body. I am the opposite, and I am so lucky that Haydeh is like me. And of anyone, she knows firsthand how bad this city is at accommodating people in wheelchairs. As I mentioned earlier, I plan what we need to get done. Things like groceries, shopping for clothes, shoes, specialty shops, dentists, doctors etc. get planned by me. And since George hates shopping of any kind, getting out to shops is NOT a piece of cake. I am blessed that Haydeh, GM or Kate are available (when they are).

Now weekends are completely different. During the summer GM takes me to his baseball games. And when the season is over, I am either bloody bored to tears (or worse). Fortunately, friends and family come for supper and to hang out. Unfortunately for the neighbours, I sit out on the deck, play my tunes, and break out into song. Surprisingly, no one has complained or moved 😊.

Having multiple sclerosis is more than *just* the loss of mobility. The swelling causes pain. Imagine if you will, an inflated balloon. Now imagine trying to fold or bend it. It is not easy. Furthermore, it is painful! Another issue is body temperature. Heat is a killer. If the temperature is anywhere above 25 degrees Celsius it means I cannot sit outside (especially in the sun), for more than 45 minutes. The sun and heat get inside me and drain me. And when I say drain me, I mean I do not even have the strength to get myself to hold a glass of water or to go to the washroom.

I know I am not the only one who suffers, I know I am not alone. Close to 80% of people afflicted with MS can associate to this temperature dysregulation. And it is not only overheating. Heat, humidity, and extreme cold trigger a bunch of weird feelings. Fortunately, I do not, but some people get blurry vision and memory or cognitive problems. Being in shade, a breeze, or being by the waterfront make a world of difference.

My body cannot acclimate as quickly or as easily as it would under normal conditions. There have been many baseball afternoon games, and other outings that I have had to forfeit. While others can drink ice water or iced tea to cool off, I cannot. I don't dare. The probability/possibility of needing to use a washroom is not a risk I can afford to take. There are not many public places and parks that have washrooms to which I can get, let alone use.

CHAPTER 13

More memories

6. The wedding dance.

I've told you all how I love to dance. Dancing is my way of letting go of emotions and other trapped feelings. The movements come from inside of me and are a pure expression of love. I have been dancing with my son since before his birth. When my belly was extended, I would place my hands under it and dance away.

I always looked forward to his wedding, the mother son dance. And when I was wheelchair bound, knowing I could not dance with him (at his wedding), well, it was like getting punched right in the throat. GM Googled and hunted for all possibilities, ways that I would be able to dance with him. He found videos. The most popular solution used by others in similar circumstances, was for him to hold me up on the dance floor. But for me, standing in the arms of my son, pretending to move to the music and hoping I would not fall, was not an option. That just was not for me. I did not know what I was going to do, but I knew making a spectacle of us was NOT going to happen. I did not want anyone's pity.

I thought and thought. Finally, I decided I was going to sing to him. When came the time for the mother son dance, GM wheeled me to the centre of the dance floor, took a chair, and sat directly in front of me. He took both my hands in his and the disc jockey cued Celine Dion's cover of Beautiful Boy. And I lip sync'd.

7. The letter

My parents fought. They fought a lot. A whole frigging lot. One fight was so bad that my father went to the basement; he sat at the desk where my sister and I used to do our homework, and he wrote a letter. At the time, I did not know to whom he was writing. (I do not remember how old I was, I think I was in grade 6 or 7.) I decided I had to get my hands on that letter. I did not know to whom it was addressed, nor what it contained. All I knew and suspected, was that it meant danger to our family. I decided if I was to do anything, it would have to be when everyone as asleep. I would have to stay awake. I could not, I wouldn't fall asleep. I was going to retrieve that letter. So that night, in order to stay awake, I talked to myself, and talked to myself, and talked to myself.

It was dark when dad came upstairs. It was well into the night. I was in the bedroom I shared with my sister. All the lights were off. I heard dad come upstairs and I heard him open in the hall closet where he kept his work clothes. I assumed he was putting the letter somewhere in there. When I (finally) heard my father snoring, when I was sure he was fast asleep, I got up quietly and went to the closet. I found the letter, and I stole it. It was addressed to his brother. I did not read it. I thought reading it was an intrusion on his privacy (apparently, I thought stealing it was ok).

The next day I heard him looking for his letter. He asked me if I had seen it - if I knew where it was. I lied. I do not think he believed me. But he did not say anything. Later that day, I got rid of the letter. I tore it into bits and flushed it.

8. Smoking

I was in college, so I must have been 17. I had been smoking (on the sly), since I was 14 or 15. I knew my mother hated it, I did not care. One day I went home not expecting her to be there. But she was. She smelled the smoke on me, and she went ballistic. She hit me until she ran out of steam. I was black and blue. Had anyone seen what she had done to me, she would have been incarcerated.

I did not try to stop her. I simply didn't care to. I felt a combination of aversion, apathy, hate, pity, disbelief, and confusion. This was not the first time my mother hit me or my sister. But on this day, I could not be bothered to react, not even try to protect myself. The feelings I was experiencing all changed into extreme defiance. I was going to make it evident that her fury was not bothering me. Trying to protect myself would have shown weakness. I would not let her know that she was hurting me. There was no way in hell I would give her that satisfaction.

I am convinced that my mother had a disorder. A big one. Her ire and short fuse could not possibly have been normal.

When my sister and I were little, if my mother discovered something broken, damaged, or soiled, she would ask each of us, who did it. I denied responsibility because I knew whatever was wrong had not been a result of anything I had done. My sister denied it because she was not going to admit it was her. My mother would slap us both. And then she would ask the question again. Again, I would deny doing anything, as would my sister. My mother would slap us again only this time a little harder. And this would go on until one of us stepped up and confessed. It did not take me long to figure out that I could save both myself and my sister from my mother's rage if I just claimed to be the guilty party right from the start.

Whereas I felt apathy, my sister did not. When my sister got older, if my mother tried anything, my sister would grab both her wrists and almost dare her to try and hit. And Marina was quite strong. So, my mother did the next best thing, she would try to kick her. I know I am painting my mother to be a horrible person. And for that I apologize. Because she was not. She was a loving person. I am sure she had demons, demons she couldn't control.

9. My MacGyver skills

I was 19 years old. I was on the way to the airport to pick up my father. He was returning from a vacation with my mom. He was returning alone, before and without my mom because he had to return to work. (My mother was not working at this point). I was on the highway headed for the airport, when the exhaust system of the car came loose. It remained attached only on at the front end. The back had come off, and it was hanging.

I pulled over and assessed the situation. I did not have a mobile phone, no one did back then; I had no way to call a tow truck. Besides, waiting for one would have made me late. I worried my father would assume I forgot to pick him up. I considered getting back into the car and continue my way to the airport, but I dismissed that option. To continue driving with the muffler hanging (and probably sparking) was not a good option. I knew with one good bump in the road it would break off completely.

I looked in the trunk of the car. Eureka! Lying there was a set of booster cables. I did what I thought would get me as far as the airport without completely losing the exhaust system. I took the cables, and I opened the back door. I put one end of the cables in the car and closed the door. Then I threw the rest of the cables under the car to the other side. I used the booster cable to lift the muffler and hold it up. I opened the other back door, put the end of the cables in that side of the car and closed the door. I created a sling which held up the fallen exhaust system.

I arrived at the airport on time to pick up my dad. When he saw what I had done, he tried to hide his smile, but I saw it. He was proud of his daughter's ingenuity.

10. Protector

Although my first multiple sclerosis episode happened after I gave birth, the more solid MS attacks did not happen until my father was dying. I have always thought that he was my protector, my buffer (from my mother). And since I was losing my protector, I guess I felt the need to become *unavailable* to and for my mother.

I was convinced that this dreaded disease made its home in my body so that I would not become my mother's keeper. I was also convinced that when my mother died, with her would go the MS. She did. It did not. Today I wonder whether my dad was my protector or whether I was his.

PART SEVEN ...

"Unexpressed emotions will never die.
They are buried alive and will come forth later
in uglier ways."
..... Sigmund Freud

CHAPTER 14
Odds and Ends

One: My mother wanted to live out her life at home. But she got dementia. The nature of her illness, and my immobility made it impossible for her to remain in her home. A huge thank you goes to George and to GM. Without them I would not have been able to give her what little I gave her. It was my sister who voiced the need for us to move her to a nursing home. And so, George and I scoured the city looking for a place for mom. I think we visited every available institution. Months later, she was moved to a residence which offered assisted living. And to the day she died, I did all I could to keep her house and her savings intact.

Two: People at work know how difficult it is for me when it is hot. And since the A/C is not too strong, they have put a fan by my desk. With MS, my body does not acclimate, I burn up from the inside out. A hot sun has the following effect...it feels like my body is melting, as would a candle or a chocolate bar left in the sun.

Three: Going to the washroom is an ordeal. I must place my feet just so, to be able to stand up without losing my balance. If my foot is half an inch too far forward or not forward enough, it means I cannot stand up and support myself. And moving backwards is terrifying and ever so difficult. I get my exercises when I need to use the washroom. I have a belt I use to return my leg to the footrest. When I transfer back into my chair, I strap the belt around my ankle and hoist my foot to the footrest. Some days it is easy. Other days I require several attempts.

Four: I experience phantom touches. At times I feel like there is a hand on my back, when in fact there isn't. Other times I must look at my hand to see where it is. Sometimes I have to verify that I am in fact still holding that piece of bread, or pen, or paper. And reaching in a pocket for something is frustrating; I cannot identify what I am feeling. Finally, sudden movements of any kind may cause dizziness and feelings of nausea.

Five: I can brush my teeth, comb my hair and put on my makeup. And whereas I can open tubes and jars, I cannot open cases which snap shut. So, I leave them open. And when a case gets closed by mistake or by mishandling, I just wait until someone is available to open it for me. As you can imagine, fastening bracelets and clasping an earring is so very exasperating. It is essential for me to be looking at what I'm doing (feeling is no longer an option). And if 2 hands are required, I need assistance.

Six: I love earrings and bracelets. Yes, I have quite a few. And by quite a few, I mean enough to wear a different set every week, for a couple of years 😄. There is a logical reason (well according to my logic anyway). I loved dressing up, looking feminine (even though I was a tomboy). I used to wear great outfits with sexy shoes. I cannot do that anymore. Wearing earrings and bracelets is my way of filling that void.

I really was what someone had labeled me, a *feminine tomboy*. I once went to a wedding reception; clad in a long evening dress, my hair was nicely coiffed -- on the back of a motorcycle. Another time I climbed onto the back of a truck I had borrowed from a colleague, to help my mother move a mattress she bought. I drove the truck to the store and in 3-inch heels (and a mini skirt I might add), I effortlessly climbed up to the truck bed, helped my dad load the mattress and tie it down.

Seven: Those who know me, know I do not quit easily. Actually, most of my 'quits' are more like time outs until I can regroup my thoughts and get reorganized. And when I cannot get all my ducks in a row, I open the gate, let them out, get new ducks and start restructuring. My latest endeavor in the quest to heal my body, consists of a combination of things. I do not care if my success will be a result of one thing, or of a combination. My goal is success. Period. My motivating mantra is a slight variation to a line from my all-time favourite movie; "as God is my witness, I'll never be unhealthy again".

Eight: I am a fan of alternative medicine and natural cures. There are many who have found help/relief/results and or cures from these wonderful alternatives. Others are die-hard believers of chemical a.k.a. traditional medicine. And whereas those drugs do good, I am not a fan. That does not mean I do not believe in traditional medication. I take my Synthroid daily, and I take antibiotics when required. I have cough syrup and acetaminophen in my medicine cabinet.

Pharmaceutical companies stand to make money by treating symptoms, not necessarily by providing cures. And the governments give researchers what I refer to as 'eternal' subsidies. So where is the motivation to find or to announce a cure? How many organizations would fold, how many people would be without jobs if tomorrow the governments stopped giving grants. That too is a subject and a conversation for another time.

Nine: I am currently following the Swank diet, reiki, and hypnosis. I am a firm believer that the body heals itself. But sometimes it needs help. We all do. Will I see results? Best case scenario, I will say good-bye to the MS. Worst case scenario, I will provide calmness to my body and my brain. And in my quest to rid myself of this disease, I have learned a lot about myself. And I have met a lot of wonderful people.

Ten: Which brings me right back to the beginning. Part of my healing strategy and homework, was to write. And as I said on the very first page, maybe someone will find comfort in reading my story, in reading what I am going through, or how I am dealing. Hopefully, someone will find answers or understanding. Hopefully, someone will find similarities, a solution, or even a friend.

Eleven: The hypnosis has brought to surface many memories. Not only memories, but also revelations. I discovered many similarities between what occurred to my mother and my grandmother, and how the details, although generations later, are quite similar. I am told these revelations are cleaning my spiritual DNA. Mine, theirs and that of future generations.

I have discovered or unwrapped significant memories and symbols, and I can reflect on how they have affected me, in the present day. Before I present more of my memories, I want to mention certain people once again. I call them my angel friends. And I'm not exaggerating when I call them angels.

Twelve: From the friend I have known the longest to my newest (aka family once removed), these angels have not just been there, but remain present in so many ways. They will actually plan and limit their outings and activities to places that they know will accommodate me, and my wheelchair.

CHAPTER 15

George

I've known George since I was 15. He was 13. His parents moved across the street and two houses down from where my family lived. He says that the first time he saw me, he told his mother that he would marry me.

George and I went to the same high school, but we were not friends. I was not interested. That did not stop him. With time, we became friends. And being Greek, he knew the customs and 'our ways' as my mother would say, so he was always welcome in our house. My mom and dad saw George as an extension of our family.

I was a member of the Greek Orthodox Church choir. And thanks to my mom, I know all the Greek folk dances. My Greek heritage is important to me. But I am and have always been more Canadian than Greek.

George and I dated other people. George and I married other people. George and I got divorced from those other people. I got divorced about a year or so earlier than George did. But our paths crossed again. One day I unexpectedly ran into George. I was walking into a shopping centre, and that same time, he was walking out. It was his birthday, so after talking for 10 minutes, I asked him if I could buy him a drink to celebrate his upcoming birthday. We continued seeing each other. Fast forward, I was 8 months pregnant when we got married.

George and I could not be more different if we tried. In everything. Food, music, hobbies, outings, activities, gift for gab, styles...you name it, we are probably on opposite ends of the spectrum. And while I was healthy, while I had my independence, it did not bother me, I did not notice it. Now though, that I have lost my autonomy, these differences are magnified. But we have history, respect, love and devotion; we make it work. And George has a big heart.

When I told George about the of the MS curse, it scared him. George felt uncomfortable and helpless. I understood his feelings. I downplayed the illness, trying to put him at ease, as much as I could anyway. And I remained independent for as long as I could.

I refer to MS it a curse because although curses are heavy, they can be reversed.

George knows, without doubt, that I am very independent. He knows my determination, and my ability to find a way to get done, what he and others claim to be impossible. George has accepted who I am, but sometimes he struggles accepting my thoughts and tenacity. And whereas I used to let that slide, I do not anymore.

I use the word tenacity instead of stubbornness☺.

Everyone has strengths. Everyone! And whereas I respect his strengths, I was wrong to downplay mine to spare his and other male egos. I have never flaunted my abilities, but I was wrong to watch someone else take credit for my thoughts and accomplishments. I disrespected myself to avoid bruising someone else's feelings. That was WRONG!

George has been right by me through my ongoing medical ordeal. Although he does not believe in all my attempts and my experiments with different forms of 'healing', he never once tried to stop me or tried to convince me otherwise. Nor has he ever complained about the thousands I have spent in the process. He knows my determination. He knows my strength and tenacity. We both know that when I heal, we will all be in a better place.

He tries to hide how he feels about what I am going through, about how it is affecting both of us. Unfortunately, when his guard is down, I hear things I wished I had not. I hear exasperation. The truth is George takes good care of me. But I know how physically difficult and uncomfortable it is at times (he is not 20 years old). And I know how bad he feels watching me struggle and suffer. Like most people in his situation, he does not know what (if anything), to do to make me feel better.

I am strong and I am defiant; but I am also struggling. And since I am not invincible there are times that my worries and woes work their way up to my face and seep out my eyes. And poor George has no idea how to deal with my pain. When my father died, it was the first time George saw me sob. He tried to console me. He could not. And I am grateful that he just let me cry.

When I have the need to cry, I do so in the shower where there are no witnesses. On one of those days, I was still weeping as I stepped out of the shower. I did not know that George was there. He saw me crying and he was convinced I needed a hug. And as he came to hug me, I saw a hesitation. He had a sudden realization that if he hugged me his clothes would get wet. I laughed. But even though I laughed, on some level that hesitation hurt me. If tables were turned, the last thing I would have thought about would be getting my clothes wet. Like I said, we could not be more different.

I know I am a burden. I know I need assistance. And for that I am truly sorry. I try to minimize all the extras George has to do because of my condition. We have hired a cleaning lady. A company has been retained to cut the grass and plow the snow. If and when home repairs are needed, I hire someone to do them. George cooks and does the groceries. He helps me get in and out of bed, in and out of the car, in and out of the shower. I am perfectly aware of and I acknowledge how much he does – things that I cannot do for or by myself. And I feel guilty. So very guilty. Not only have I lost 20 years of my life, but I've also cost him 20 years of his. (We do have plans to get a new shower, one that doesn't have a step).

I thank the Lord it's me and not of one of my loved ones who has this disease. But if they did, I know I would be very present for them.

My mother had dementia. And even from my wheelchair I did all I could. Before she was placed in an assisted living facility, I took care of everything I could. I would call her 3 times a day and talk her through every step required for her to heat her meals and take her medication. And I paid all her bills which at first was not as easy as one might think.

When my mother received any bills, bills she felt were unjust (such as municipal taxes, or school taxes, electricity, heating etc.), she would write a note on the bill explaining why she felt warranted *not* to pay it, and mail that bill right back to the sender. When I discovered what she was doing I had all her mail rerouted to my house. I can laugh about it now, but it was stressful in the beginning as I had to do all this behind her back. Had she known; she would have never agreed. Relinquishing control to her was worse than death.

One day we were taking my mother out for a ride. I mentioned something about my school taxes. My mother informed me that she too received her tax bill, and she returned it to the school board with a stern note, listing reasons why she should not be required to pay school taxes.

I could not get into my mother's house, there were steps I couldn't climb. So, George had to handle everything there which required physical interaction. The first thing that had to be done, was to remove all the fuses on her stove. I did not take any chances of her burning down the place. We (George) started cooking for her and preparing meals for which all she had to do was to place in the microwave to heat. Unfortunately cooking for her and preparing her meals did not last long. My mother was convinced we were poisoning her.

Paranoia is part of dementia, the illness from which she suffered. So, since she would not eat anything we made, off to our local grocer George went to buy single serving homemade meals. He would go pick up 21 meals a week (3 meals a day for 7 days). Every week, he would buy 21 meals, take them to her house and put them in the fridge and freezer. He would pick her up on weekends and we would take her out to a mall, or for coffee, or to a park. (Eventually GM took over that duty).

One day George told me there was not any room in her freezer for the meals we had bought. That didn't make sense. I questioned my mom. She said she did not know why. I asked her if she was eating properly, and she said yes. Any way I looked at it, it made no sense. I used to call her 3 times every day, every day, and I used to step her through taking her pills and preparing her meals by putting them in the microwave, even what setting to choose.

I would tell her which pills she needed to take, where the pills were, where the glasses were. And I would tell her where to put away the remaining pills so I could tell her where to find them later. I would ask her which meal she wanted to eat, what setting to select on the microwave, and listen for the bell on the microwave indicating the food was ready.

Now George was telling me there was no room in the freezer. Something did not fit. Then it hit me! I asked her if she was squirreling away food, if she afraid that we wouldn't bring more and that she would go hungry. In a low, almost scared voice, she said yes. Poor soul. I had to reassure her we would always take care of her.

When she was at the residence, George would take me there after work so I could feed her. She had developed dysphagia, a common occurrence with dementia sufferers. She had forgotten how to swallow. The staff could not sit and feed her. And I was not going to leave her hungry. And although there were days, where she was not sure of who I was, she knew I was someone familiar, someone whom she knew and who knew her.

George understood how important it was to me to take care of my mother, and although he is extremely uncomfortable being around sick or old people, he would take me to her. When my dad was in the hospital it was different. I was healthy. I could drive myself and do whatever I had to do for him. And taking care of my dad was easier because I did not have to plan anything for him; dad just required more of *me*, more of my presence. I was doing things for dad that nurses would not. When an orderly was available, they would call for one, otherwise it was me who was available.

CHAPTER 16

Get more memories

11. Death

I'm guessing that the death of my mother's brother (more precisely how my grandmother reacted to that horrifying execution), marked my mother severely. As I mentioned earlier, seeing everything in her house draped in black left her a great disdain for that colour. But more - my mother played on the doom of death and its finality for almost everything.

A disturbing memory is how often she needed reassurance that when she died, that my sister and I would visit her grave with flowers. The particularly distressing factor in all this was how young we were when she started these guilt / control trips. We still lived on Clarke Street, so I had to be under 5 years old.

I had learned, at a very early age to shut out my mother. (I must have been born with an old soul). I ignored many of her scare tactics and her 'pity me' shenanigans. What they did to my subconscious however is another story.

12. The Pink dress

I am convinced my mother was battling demons of various sort. Either that, or she really could not handle stress. We had a social event to attend. Because of the pink dress I was wearing, I am guessing it was a wedding. I must have been about 4. My mother first dressed me and then my sister, and while she and my dad were getting ready, I went outside. I promised to stay clean. I was wearing a pink dress with a thin dark brown velvet belt, sash style.

One of the neighbour kids had a box of candy covered black licorice. I asked her for one and she refused. I obviously said something because she spit on me what was in her mouth. *NO!* I had this blob of black, right smack in the middle of my pink dress. Worse, I had to go inside and show my mother. My terror was not in vain. I will not get into details, but it wasn't pleasant.

> *I do not know if it has anything to do with the event, but if I have to go somewhere now, I'm still putting on final touches as I am walking out the door. I am never the first to be ready. Oh, and guess what colour I like least* 😠

13. Head strong

I have not met anyone as headstrong as my mother. Oops, wrong. Apart from my sister, I have not met anyone as headstrong as my mother. Oops, wait. Although not at the same level, I think I too qualify in the head strong category.

When my mother had a notion, or a point of view, or a comment, (or an itch), it was not kept in her back pocket. And she would not back off nor would she ease up. She would go on and on - and on - until the other person gave in or walked away. And depending on who and where or what, walking away did not signify the end of it. She would continue. My mother would proudly admit, her own words "if God himself told me I was wrong, I'd look him straight in the eye and tell him NO, *YOU* are".

I admit it, I am quite headstrong. My determination is part of my strength. I cannot tolerate being lied to or told something cannot be done - when I know it can. I am not good at rolling over and playing dead. But I will not argue a point for the mere satisfaction of being right. And whereas I shut out my mother or walked away from confrontation with her, (and eventually others), I do not do that anymore.

I walked away from altercations in the past. It was more important for me to keep the peace and spare people's feelings. But unfortunately, I did not walk away clean. I kept everything buried inside. Not anymore. Family, friend, or person of authority; if you show me no respect, I extend you the same discourtesy. Deal with it.

14. Ugly shoes

In my whole life, I do not remember (and even though I say I don't remember, I am certain beyond a shadow of a doubt), I don't ever remember my father ever *purposely* going out to buy me (or my sister or my mother) a birthday or Christmas gift. Not that he did not pay for things. Neither was it because he was heartless; he just never took the time to go and buy something or surprise us with anything for any occasion.

One year, it was Christmas morning, he asked me if I remembered to buy something for my mother. Really dad? You remembered to ask me.... the day of! Really??

I was 16. I had a part time weekend job. I was saving up for a new pair of shoes. I mentioned it to my dad and (*shock*), he said he would take me to find shoes, AND – that he would buy them for me. Wait, what?

Earlier I told you how much I love shoes. And not just plain shoes. I love funky, sexy, out of the ordinary shoes. Always did. Dad had meat and potatoes taste. And he wanted to select my shoes. I suspect because he knew he would not afford the shoes I would have chosen. I could have opted to pay the difference, and buy the shoes I wanted, but that would have bruised his ego. Plus, this was the first gift from him. And it was not even a special occasion, it wasn't a holiday, or my birthday. I was not going to let anything prevent it from happening. So, he chose and bought the shoes. The ugliest pair of shoes in the whole store.

I wore them. It gave my dad such great pleasure to have bought me these shoes. These ugly shoes. There was no way in hell I would hurt him by telling him I did not like them. So, I wore them. And damn it he was right about them being sturdy. Those damn shoes would not wear out. *ARGH.*

Many years later, I would buy my dad shoes. Which he loved. And he wore them, and wore them, and wore them. He never knew it, but his shoes cost me more than the combined monetary equivalent of all the shoes he had ever owned in the past.

I don't remember any of it, but I have on many occasions heard the story about the time my dad went to Canadian Tire to buy things he needed for the car. To save money, he did all his mechanical work himself. I was with him and I saw a bicycle. He says I ran to it, jumped on it and was so proud of not falling. It had training wheels on and was affixed on the rack ☺. He said my excitement and the look on my face was killing him, he did not have the heart to take me off that bike. So he bought it for me. It was a metallic blue. And although I outgrew it in a few years, I kept it for a very, very long time. And you guessed it. My favourite colour is blue.

CHAPTER 17

Dealing

You hear of couples who have to deal with health issues / situations; partners who are faced with decisions of what it comes down to, as fight or flight. There are those who do not stay in the marriage, those for whom 'love' is contingent to what's in it for them. My knee jerk reaction was the same as most others' – simply, that these people are assholes.

Today though, I do not think that at all. Every relationship either works or it does not. There are factors that make it so. And while certain situations or scenarios make conditions acceptable or bearable, others make them worse. And something that was ready to break, suddenly does.

In different ways, things are as difficult for the healthy partner, as they are difficult for the other. Trust me, I know. The one, and in my opinion, only 'fortunate' part to this disease, is that the dependence and requirements for help were not an overnight thing. The changes were gradual which technically gave both partners time to adjust and to make adjustments. However, preexisting personality differences between the two partners become ever so much more prominent, and the chips start making loud noises when they fall.

The pains are real. Some are visible, others are not. Some are physical, some are emotional, some are psychological. As with anything, circumstances determine the degree in which each individual experiences these aches, and heartaches. Some people like to talk about what they are going through. Doing so helps them deal. I was/am an extremely private person. This book would not have been written was it not for my latest therapy. I do not believe in speaking about what bothers me. I do not want to show (what I consider to be) vulnerability. And I do not want sympathy or pity. It is a good thing I'm not an alcoholic. I would have sucked at AA meetings.

The truth is, I am surprised at how much I enjoy(ed) writing this book. I am surprised at the memories which have surfaced, of which you have read only a few. Maybe one day I will write a book based only on memories. Then again, probably not.

I have discovered that whereas it is ok (or tolerated) to be intelligent when you are healthy, it is almost 'expected' that your intelligence diminishes with the loss of your mobility. Let me explain. I am not a dummy, and in many ways I am self-sufficient. Whereas I did many things independently, I now need assistance. That does not mean though, that because I cannot physically do some things, that I do not know how they could be done, or even that they could be done. Regrettably, and maybe it is the wheelchair, for some reason, when certain people look at me, I don't fit their image of *how* I should think.

Firstly. Yes, I am in a wheelchair. Being in a wheelchair means I have mobility issues. My brain works! My mobility has not - I repeat NOT - affected my I.Q. or my analytical abilities. Some might say that when there is a loss of one ability, the remaining abilities get honed, almost making up for what is lost.

Secondly. I am 57 years old (give or take 😊). Intelligence does not go down as age goes up. Quite the opposite. I have seen more, experienced more, and learned more things. I am not suffering any memory lapses, nor do I suffer from Dementia or Alzheimer's etc.

Thirdly. I am a woman. And while many women have attained significant achievements in many disciplines, there remain stains/stigma/ stupidity concerning the 'weaker' sex. It is sad, but it is true.

I may have three x's. Three x's, three o's, who cares. I am not playing tic - tack - toe. I am who I am. And whereas I have made mistakes in my life, I have accomplished much. And I'm not done 😉

PART EIGHT ...

"When you heal trauma, you heal the nervous system.
When you heal the nervous system,
you heal the emotional body.
When you heal the emotional body,
you heal the psychic body.
When you heal the psychic body, you heal the vibration.
Once the vibration is healed, realities change."
..... Angie

CHAPTER 18

Revelations

I shake my head at how convinced I was that I knew myself. After all, I have lived with myself for decades. I should know me. Right? Wrong! In my case anyway, I was wrong.

I do not know at what point I shut out the truth and let my analytical mind or another part of my brain take over. It is with / through my latest healing, that I opened my eyes (so to speak). Everyone has a dominant strength or sense. In my case my dominant sense is my emotional side. As much as I can remember things that happened, the facts, I was controlled by and responded to how a particular event made me feel. And when the feelings were too much to handle, I just shut everything down.

The body is brilliant that way. It fights infection with white blood cells and a fever. We cough to fight to clear our passages of foreign objects. And in my case when my emotions were too much for me to handle, my system suppressed them. I guess this was better solution than trying to cope by turning to drugs or alcohol.

Dancing

I have said it before, I'll say it again, I LOVE, LOVE, LOVE dancing. Ever since I could remember (and through stories I have heard), I had the dance bug / rhythm / talent, since before I was born. But it was not until a healing session with my therapist Isabelle, that I had the revelation (I don't know why I didn't see it before); every emotion I suppressed, every frustration I hid, every anger hurt and pain I stifled, was released and came free when I dance(d).

I always knew how much I loved to dance, but I never realized or understood why. To this day when I hear music, any kind of music, magic happens. My emotions not only surface, but they also gush out. Like a cork explodes open on a bottle of champagne, or like the contents burst forth from a shaken can of soda, nothing is able to hold them back.

And since I am (was) a good dancer, I never even considered there could be an underlying reason to my passion. How ironic is it (*or is it*), that my mother, one of the causes, perhaps even the prime cause of my frustration, was the one who taught me to dance, folk dancing, ballroom dancing, social dancing. It was her who got me started with ballet classes at the age of 4.

Both parents were good dancers, my mother however was a fantastic dancer.

Fear

I am strong. Not physically, but strong when it comes to handling fear. And I do not intimate easily. I am the one who handled and handles blood, gore, and pain for my family and friends. And I do so with compassion. If a member of my family or a friend is scared or troubled, I am the one who stands (pardon the irony) by them and offers a hand, or an ear or whatever help I could offer, regardless my state.

Once again though, during therapy I discovered something more about myself. I told you about my Yiayia Helen and the spiritual visitations she had, and how I shared or inherited her ability to see spirits and entities. Well, when I was a little girl, one of these visitations/episodes scared me. I did not know why or how it happened, I didn't know who the entity was or what she wanted, but she scared me. Scared me right into silence. Scared me enough that I did not even tell my dad. And until recently, I had no idea to what extent I had been scared.

My mother

My mother had a serious problem. I suspected she was either bipolar or she had a split personality. I knew her life with my dad was *not* a match made in heaven and I knew how financially stressful her days were.

My mother worked hard. She scrimped and saved so that we would not be seen as poor. As I got older, I excused her fits of rage and tantrums; I assumed they were a result of this stress and loneliness, or a psychological illness. But to a child, logical analysis is useless. A child needs a loving mommy, one to whom she can run to and feel protected.

I loved my mom, but I never considered her a friend. She was never 'mommy'. She was a very strong woman who taught me a ton! When I was old enough, I traveled with her, we went shopping, went to restaurants and shows. I repeat, I loved her, but I was not emotionally close. I know now how much I missed that.

I owe my mother an apology, at the very least I owe her compassion. She could not give me what she did not know. She was telling the truth (her truth) when she referred to me as her sister, her friend, her confidant etc. That is exactly how she saw me. My poor mother never had a childhood. Circumstances made her grow up in a huge hurry. She did not have a real childhood. And far too soon, she became the bread winner and the caregiver to her mother.

Poor mom lost her dad before she saw her second birthday and lost her brother before she was in double digits. She had to think and act like an adult to survive during German occupation (WWII). By the time she reached her teens she was in Athens studying and working and supporting her mom. She did not know how to see a child - as a child. She could not give me what she did not know.

Poor sweet mom didn't experience a normal childhood, she didn't have a man who valued her or loved her, not the way she was expecting to be loved and cared for.

CHAPTER 19

Acceptance

I finally understood the importance of acceptance and how important it is to focus only on the good. Accepting does not mean giving up, it simply (and actually) means *accepting*. Our brains like the feeling associated with acceptance and find/give us more to feel good about.

The word acceptance holds so much meaning. Looking back, taking apart and peeling back my memories and experiences, things are now so clear (*ding, ding, ding*). I never accepted myself. Did it start when I heard my mother apologize to my father that I was not (born) a boy? Possibly. Could be. Maybe. Bottom line is I never accepted myself.

Striving to be better, to do better, to succeed, those are all good things. Doing so to gain acceptance, however, is NOT the best of reasons.

How could I have expected anyone to accept me or respect me, or even take me seriously, when I did not accept myself. *What the ---.* How did I not see this before? Seriously, how did I not. I pride myself on my intelligence and my analytical skills, yet this little (humungous) detail eluded me.

I must have known. Why else did I have such drive to push forward. Though, I didn't push forward. I incessantly but quietly inched forward, as I did not want to bring any attention to myself.

The brain is amazing. I mean my brain knew all along that I wanted, that I needed to be noticed. And guess what. With the MS, I am being noticed. Mission accomplished. I am being noticed, but for the wrong reasons. Whereas I am taking up room, getting very noticed, I am being noticed primarily for my physical handicap.

Ok brain. I get it.

On somedays, my mom's teachings ring so loudly in my ears. And for every good piece of advice she gave me, she immediately said something to cancel her initial statement, and she created a dichotomy.

Be careful, do not trust anyone.

Trust me always, I only want what is best for you.
Only I know what's best for you

Use your brain. Do what you think is best.

Listen to what others tell you. They have experience.

Be with someone better.

Be with someone from your class or background.
Stick with what you know.

A woman can do whatever she wants.

Why do women want equality?
What makes women think they are as capable as a man?

Be independent.

A woman without a man, is nothing.

Save for your golden years. If you do not look after yourself no one will.

Family is everything.
It is a family's responsibility to take care of one another.

CHAPTER 20

Anger and Acceptance

I used to feel anger. And that anger would last a long time. I used to feel so much irritation that sometimes those feelings turned into feelings of internal rage. But now, I feel nothing.

Am I accepting, or am I suppressing? Am I accepting the choices I have made? Am I now dealing with the consequences of those choices? That is what we are supposed to do. Isn't it? Accept what is, for what it is. The anger has faded. In its stead, often, I feel ... a void. I feel nothing. Is feeling nothing acceptance? Is that how I am supposed to feel?

Not feeling anger, or defiance; not feeling anything, *usually* means I have shut down. I've shut off my feelings. I simply do not care. I do not care if I hear any excuses or reasons or justifications or anything else for that matter. My energy is closed. No anger or defiance, I simply feel - done, I feel indifference. Is that acceptance?

From what I have read and from what I have been told, acceptance is the doorway to healing. So, am I accepting? Or am I once again shutting out feelings? I cannot differentiate between feelings of acceptance with turning off as to not feel disappointment. So, Is turning off a step in the right direction? If I am immobilizing pain, am I immobilizing the source of this pain, and its ability to hurt me.

"I do not blindly accept
the things I cannot change,
I try to change
the things I don't want to accept."
….. Unknown

CHAPTER 21

Suffering and Acceptance

"If you resist change, you resist life."

-Sadhguru

Buddhist philosophy says that "Suffering is pain multiplied by resistance". Essentially, accepting the pain (multiple sclerosis in my case) causes less suffering than struggling vainly against it. I hate that word, *vainly*.

According to this philosophy, I have a choice. My not so self-serving reaction is telling me my choice is opting between a rock and a hard place.

If I properly understand the explanation given in Buddhism, rejecting the fact I have multiple sclerosis, causes me pain. But I know I have MS; I am not rejecting that fact. I do not dispute it either.

I fully understand what medical professionals say, that there is no cure. Is my desire to find a way to cure myself of this disease wrong? And the fact that I haven't been able to *yet*, is it that which is causing me pain?

There was 'no cure' to many diseases, until the cure was found.

I strongly believe there is a way to control this disease. Although there is no *cure* yet which can be prescribed in pill or injection form, I want to believe a cure exists. Doctors and medicine just go so far, and then the breakthrough is announced with great joy. And maybe I will not find my answers, but I will not quit. My search for this elusive cure is *precisely* because I accept the fact that I have MS and I want to help me and others who are struggling/dealing with it.

How do I get my brain to understand or even differentiate that wanting a better life, a healthy life, is not a control issue.

I have grey hair, and I choose to dye it. When I want to shed some pounds, I choose to monitor my caloric intake. If I break a bone, I get it reset. Taking control of these situations, taking action in these cases, is perfectly acceptable. These choices and actions are not frowned upon or considered as negative control issues.

I am told that acceptance is "the key that unlocks the door to happiness". So what does acceptance really mean. I have heard some say that accepting a situation or condition is taking the *"ok, so what"* approach. Hmmm... I do not see it like that. Whereas I *accept* the fact that a bully can do me harm, I am smart enough to avoid a situation which would put me in that bully's path. I will not take the "ok, so what" approach. I will make a decisive effort to keep me out of harm's way.

I do not want pain, nor do I choose it. And I am not resisting or rejecting MS. Quite the opposite. I have firsthand knowledge what multiple sclerosis can do to a body, how it can change the life of its victim, and those around him or her. I accept what I have. But it does not mean I have to give up or give in.

I am not obsessed. I am not losing sleep looking for an answer. I do not spend hours consumed looking for a solution, a cure. Neither do I host pity parties. I have MS. I know it. I have accepted it. And yes, of course there are times that my immobility and my dependence on another are very difficult and bothersome.

I can acknowledge and accept, make the best of my time, or I can spend most of my life moping (woe is me). Those who know me know that feeling sorry for myself is not my style. Acceptance requires effort and determination. I have never shied from either of these. I am not about to now.

I have accepted my diagnosis. That does not mean I will let go of the quest to improve or change things, (specifically my condition). I do not ever want to lose that drive; I don't ever want to detach from that hope. Nor do I want to give up. And yes, I do know there are times I have to let go, and accept defeat.

Those who know me well, know that to me, defeat means a dead end only after no stone has been left unturned. At which time I tell myself to Let go and let God.

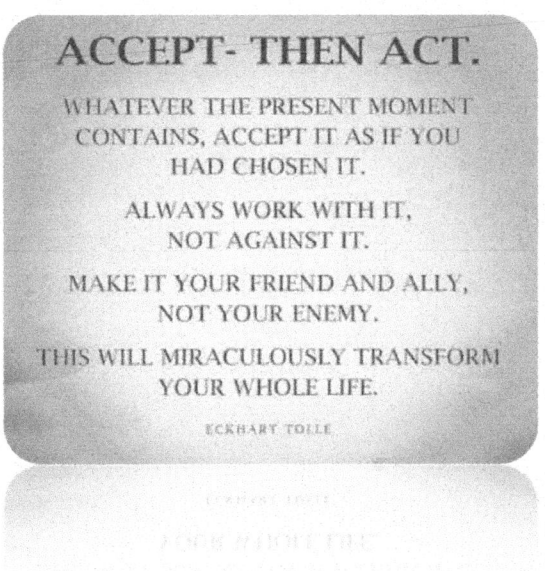

ACCEPT- THEN ACT.

WHATEVER THE PRESENT MOMENT CONTAINS, ACCEPT IT AS IF YOU HAD CHOSEN IT.

ALWAYS WORK WITH IT, NOT AGAINST IT.

MAKE IT YOUR FRIEND AND ALLY, NOT YOUR ENEMY.

THIS WILL MIRACULOUSLY TRANSFORM YOUR WHOLE LIFE.

ECKHART TOLLE

I remember something I was taught early in my 20s, "if by worrying you can change the outcome, then by all means knock yourself out". Worry does not change the future it just robs us of the present.

I assure you; I am not worrying.

PART NINE ...

"God, grant me the serenity to stop beating
myself up for not doing things perfectly,
the courage to forgive myself because
I'm working on doing better,
and the wisdom to love me, to love myself just the way I am".
..... Unknown

CHAPTER 22

Good is born of Bad

Up – Down – Up – Down. My life has been a series of ups and downs, a seesaw. To the point that I am afraid to be happy, to rejoice or to even plan. I am afraid that I will jinx my good fortune. It has been brought to my attention that I could be subconsciously self-sabotaging. If this is true, I want to make it stop.

Here is a rundown.

- *I got married (love) .... 6 months later the marriage was over*
- *I landed a great job .... 2 years later the division in which I worked was transferred to Toronto*
- *1 found another great job .... that division got closed in Canada*
- *I wanted a child....it took me 3 years to conceive*
- *We bought a house....my husband lost his job, and the car which came with that job*
- *I gave birth to my beautiful son .... I experienced my first MS attack*

- *I had a good job …. I lost it, and I was the prime breadwinner*
- *I found a new job …. I was loved by my immediate manager, but she changed careers and her replacement saw me as a threat and got rid of me, (but not before stealing all my ideas)*
- *Next job …. I was appreciated by everyone with whom I interacted, but it wasn't a full-time job, I lost 40% of my earnings*
- *my son was 10 years old, playing baseball, taking tennis lessons, things were settling nicely …… my father suffered a heart attack and died a few months later. The MS got worse*

I have heard people use these two statements

- 'never a good without a bad'
- 'something good is born from something bad'

I used to wonder why, when everything was going well for me, why something happened to quash my happiness and my progress. Isabelle, my therapist, suggested to me that I might be looking at it all wrong. Instead of looking at the unfavorable or unfortunate side of what happened, I should look at what good sprung forward from the uncomfortable position I was in. I thought that was an interesting angle, I wanted to give it a try.

Situation:

- *We bought a house….my husband lost his job…. what horrible luck*
- when we decided to buy our house, after budgeting to the penny, a week before signing for a mortgage I found out I

156

was pregnant. I would need money for the baby, furnishings, baby clothes, and full salary (not maternity leave) to pay the mortgage. Where was the money going to come from? Additionally, my husband lost his job. Argh!

Flipping that thought would be something like ....

- *What joy! After all the time it took me to conceive my sweet baby, it happened on time for him to be in a new home.*

I have decided to revisit my roller coaster ride and exploring each incident from a positive vantage.

> *life isn't finding shelter in the storm.*
> *It's about learning to dance in the rain.*
> *..... Sherrilyn Kenyon*

CHAPTER 23

Holidays

Easter, by all accounts is the major holiday of the Greek Orthodox religion. And growing up, at our house, it was so. Mom cooked and baked for Christmas, but nothing like the baking and cooking she did for Easter.

Resurrection was a huge deal. We would get dressed and go to Church were we stayed until the priest presented the holy light and sang Xristos Anesti (Christ has risen). Greek Orthodox people, whether regular church goers or not, went to Church for the resurrection. They just did, they still do. As you can imagine the churches on this night were and are packed, and people spill out into the street for blocks.

As a little girl I felt sorry for people who had residence near the church. They had to endure noise and chanting past midnight, and until the crowds dispersed.

When my parents were alive, St George's Cathedral was their parish church. It was also mine while I was growing up. It was there that I was a member of the choir for years. But years later, I had my own family and although I still attended Sunday services at St. George, it made better sense to attend resurrection at Greek Orthodox Church of Saints Constantine and Helen, the church near my home. The church was a mere 10 minutes from my home, and the parking was so much better/easier.

I assumed the cooking and baking rituals; it was time to have the holiday celebration and family gathering at my house. But my mother would have none of it. Her church was suddenly more important than her family. In fact, it had nothing to do with the choice of where we would attend service, it was nothing more than a control issue for her. And whereas I didn't give a rat's ass whether she celebrated Easter at my house, she kept my father from joining us.

Her antics and tantrums did not sit well with me. But I never put my father in a situation where he had to choose where and how he would celebrate Easter. I knew all too well what his life would be like back at his house if he celebrated Easter with us. Still, dad made an appearance. He would stay for minutes, and he would excuse my mother's absence stating she had a bad headache.

Christmas is absolutely, positively, my favourite of the holidays. It always has been. I cannot say why. It is not because fond memories of Christmas when I was growing up, that's for damn sure. When I was a little girl, Christmas gifts were essentials, things we needed; socks, mittens, p.j.'s.

Yet I have always loved Christmas. The smiles on people's faces, the feelings of happiness, the generosity and sharing. Mom would always take me and my sister to the Santa Claus parade and then we would follow Santa on to the department store, Eaton's. I loved the parades. It didn't matter how cold it was or how much snow was on the ground. I loved going to the Santa Claus parade, loved watching the brightly coloured floats, the jesters and polar bears, the clowns and especially the marching bands. The Christmas tunes they played made me smile. And when the drummers went by, I would feel the booming right through my body. I felt the vibrations in my heart.

Once inside Eaton's, (the Canadian equivalent of Macy's), we would line up to be photographed with Santa. That was a big deal. Although the cost was not huge, it was an extra expense. But my mom always made sure to have money available for the photo. It was important to her that we would have those memories. And I am grateful that she did. Once we reached our teen years, my sister and I continued taking a photo with Kris Kringle. (I have photos with him from the time I was 4 to the time I was 18).

Poor mom could not afford toys or anything frivolous (she was already finding the means to pay for my ballet lessons). Toys just were not in the budget. So, before we got to see Santa, we were well instructed. When the man in red asked what we wanted for Christmas, we would politely tell him that we wanted mittens, or whatever else mom thought was practical and which she had already bought.

Did I mention? My parents fought a lot. And the holiday period was no exception. I do not know if the fights got worse during the holidays or if I just noticed them more. Still, as much as I hated the fighting, the yelling, screaming, and cursing that was going on around me, I did not let it spoil my Christmas.

When we were little, despite what and how my parents felt about each other, they would put their differences aside and make Christmas Eve special for my sister and me. We lived in a house which had no fireplace, no chimney. I always wondered, and worried that Santa would not be able to get in. On Christmas Eve my father would take me and my sister into the kitchen and tell us that Santa would soon come and that we had to be sweet and polite.

I learned to hate the word 'polite'. All my life I was told to be polite. It didn't matter the circumstances, nor did it matter how I felt. I had to be polite. And to my parents (especially my mother), polite did not mean that I had to choose my words carefully. It meant I had to shut my mouth and walk away. I had to be submissive.

Of course, during the time my father was talking to us about Santa's pending arrival, my mother would take the gifts from where she had hidden them and place them under the tree. By the time dad ended his talk, Santa had come, and we had missed seeing him. Every year dad would take us into the kitchen and would give us his annual Christmas talk. I remember thinking to myself "hurry up dad, or we'll miss Santa again this year". But if course, I said nothing. I was being *polite*.

By 6 or 7 years old I knew there was no Santa. But Christmas remained such a special time of year. Having a Greek mother, the holidays were even more reason to follow Greek traditions. Especially the cooking and baking. And dear Lord was that woman a fantastic chef and baker. To date only 2 people I know can meet her talents. My sister is one. My friend Mary's mother is the other.

When I started working, nothing gave me more pleasure than to buy gifts for my family and friends. I would listen and observe, until I knew what they liked and wanted. And I would budget throughout the year for these gifts. Then I would wrap them lovingly and hide them in my closet or under my bed.

We were not rich. But my parents taught me the importance of helping people who were less fortunate than us. Mom never threw out any clothing we outgrew. She washed and ironed what we no longer wore, and she gave them to families who had even less than we did.

Funny story: when I had my son, I taught him, at an early age, the importance of sharing. Every year at Christmas time, I made him pick one of his toys and we would give it to charity. Of course, I would replace what he chose to donate. And I would match the value of the toy given. So, if he decided to give away something insignificant, he got an insignificant something in return.

One year as he was deciding on what he was going to donate, he looked at me and asked me why HE had to give something for another child. Wasn't that what Santa was supposed to do?

Yikes. I was not expecting that question from a 4-year-old. I thought fast and told him Santa could not afford toys for all the children in the world. I told him that parents gave Santa money for him to buy gifts. But some parents did not have any money, so we had to help. I don't know if he believed me, but the subject was dropped.

Now I prepare for Christmas with the physical limitations MS has forced upon me. How things have changed. Christmas is still my favourite holiday, but now I am dependent on others to recreate the

Christmas' that live in my heart and in my head. God love GM and Haydeh, they take the time to take me Christmas shopping. And I am extremely grateful! Sadly though, I cannot get out when I want. I fully acknowledge that people have their own lives, family obligations and responsibilities. Their availability is not guaranteed. And so, I shop when I can.

In our house, the season of celebrations starts with a Christmas tree decorating party. The tree is decorated differently every year. Everyone pitches in. I have a lot of decorations. I still have some of my parent's special ornaments, and in 30 years I have amassed so many more. I used to go out the week after Christmas, and take advantage of boxing week sales and purchase gorgeous ornaments. I am glad I did because that too is now but a memory.

Christmas baking has taken a beating. I do rely on poor George to bake. And being in the kitchen is not his thing. I look for simple recipes with which cookies could be made with minimal fuss and effort. Still, I feel guilty asking him to give up some of his free(er) time to bake Christmas goodies (even though he enjoys devouring them). Friends bring me what they bake. And although I love their thoughtfulness and kindness, I feel bad that I cannot reciprocate. I feel very uncomfortable.

Christmas shopping has changed to adapt to the limitations MS has launched. A good deal of my shopping is done online (thank you technology). So, I buy throughout the year, starting as early as January. My den doubles as gift storage area. I know what I buy. However, (and this a big however), George puts the purchases away. Come November/December, locating the purchases I know I have made, brings about .... frustration. Even though each box or package is clearly marked as to its respective contents, when boxes are stacked one atop another, they must be moved and rearranged to find what's what – and where. And as do most shoppers, I purchase extra gifts to be used for last minute hostess gifts or to fill the 'oopsie' forgotten on Santa's list. Non shoppers a.k.a. George, do not understand this.

That is just a glimpse of how multiple sclerosis has altered my Christmas'. Unfortunately, there is more. In my case, wrapping gifts takes the prize. When I was well and able, wrapping (a gift), was just as important as the thought that went into the purchase of that gift. The paper, the ribbon and the tag were thought and picked out with as much love and care. My creative side loved this stage of gifting. But now, I need George to wrap things. Yikes! Major yikes!

Instead of buying wrapping paper and boxes, I now buy loads of tissue paper and gift bags. Unfortunately, ribbons are pretty much a thing of the past. And the tags now just read *To and From*. No more cute notes, or clues pertaining to the contents of the package. My friends and family understand. And so do I. I have accepted it. But I am not a happy camper.

My friend Johanne is a master at gift wrapping. She even uses old costume jewelry to adorn her packages.

I am one of the few people who still sends out Christmas cards. Although I cover many friends with private messages using social media, I still send cards to my longtime friends. I can no longer hold a pen well enough to write a personal message, so I prepare 3 sets of labels using my computer: (i) my return address, (ii) the recipient's address and (iii) the message which will be put inside the card. And once again, I depend on George to put everything together and get the cards out to friends and neighbours. More guilt.

There is no doubt, MS has robbed me of many freedoms and certain pleasures. But I have replaced and substituted getting things done by implementing certain shortcuts. I cannot avoid being dependent on someone to help … which I truly appreciate. But I harbour and endure the accompanying feelings of imposition.

PART TEN ...

"There comes a point when you either embrace who and what you are, or condemn yourself to be miserable all your days. Other people will try to make you miserable; don't help them by doing the job yourself.
..... Laurell K. Hamilton

CHAPTER 24

Feelings of Anger

Joanna, one of the beautiful persons who has been helping me heal spiritually, asked me if I had considered grief management. Before she had a chance to finish asking her question (which was really a suggestion), I heard myself tell her that I did not need grief management. Woah! *Ding, Ding, Ding.* If that was not my defenses shooting double barreled, I do not know what it was.

I am stubborn, but I'm not stupid. I realized, by the speed of my defensive reply and my defiance, that grief management was possibly or probably something I needed. Obviously, my subconscious mind had something buried that wanted (and did not want) to be uncovered and dealt with.

And so, I tried grief management, which by the way is quite expensive. After I introduced myself and gave Lori (the grief management specialist) a brief history of myself, she asked me what I wanted to discuss, what I wanted her to help me through.

I had no idea. I honestly did not know what it was, which memor(ies) or event(s) for which I required her help and guidance. I seriously had no clue. I did know however, by my reaction to the suggestion of grief management, that something big was waiting to be uncovered. I felt uncomfortable. Lori asked me a series of questions We chatted some more. I earnestly hunted for something to discuss with the grief counselor. Nothing was surfacing. I had no idea, absolutely none, what it was, the issue or issues which required healing. To respond to her questions, I went through more of my childhood history. Yuk! Additional ugly memories surfaced. But nothing for which, I felt, needed further attention.

Unfortunately, after a few more appointments, I was no closer to knowing what 'grief' needed to be dealt with. Booking more appointments was useless .... I had no idea what I wanted to discuss; I was no closer to identifying what was giving me grief. Argh. Our budget confirmed I could not just keep talking. I decided to minimize the number of follow up appointments.

Another part of my healing therapy was to answer five questions. (Joanna had given me homework. It was unclear to me, but obviously she knew what she was doing). She gave me five questions. And every day, I had to give different answers to the same five questions. By the end of week two, the frustration was undeniable. How many times can anyone provide a different answer to the same stupid five questions. Argh!

And then it happened. Something inside me unlocked. I realized I harboured anger. And distrust. But of what? What was I not seeing??

A couple of days into week three of this (homework), I woke up and I had an answer. And the answer shocked me. It floored me. I had dreamed of my father, and my mother. I remember the dream was illogical, it was weird. I did not remember the details - but I remembered the revelation. I FELT A BIG DISTRUST OF MEN.

Never would I have thought that. And yet, reviewing my history of and with the men in my life, it kind of made sense. Or was I reaching. And my MS flared when my father died. Could it be that I felt like the man I loved so much, had abandoned me.

My grandmother, she lost her husband and her son.
Genetic memories?

I did and did not understand what was happening? I am not one to express emotion. I do not share my private side, my feelings – obviously not even to myself. Yet I am now writing about them. Not only did I reach the inner me, but I am sharing these depths with you. If nothing else, am I healing my soul.

When I started writing this book, I was a very pleasant person; a bubbly personality, with a happy smile and a bounce in my voice so to speak. I still have a pleasant and bubbly personality, a happy smile, and a bounce in my voice. So, what has changed? LOTS!

What I was before, was staged. And I was good at it. So good at it that I had fooled myself. I was not forcing anything, but I was staging most of it. Part of me went with the concept 'fake it until you make it'. Now that I think about it, it was more like 'fake it until you feel it'. And I was so good at it, that I had convinced even myself of this makeshift reality.

171

I have always been pleasant, happy, and vibrant. I was making a conscious effort to continue being so. I did not want anyone to see the grey or dark feelings. Primarily because I did not want to talk about what had or was wounding me. At times I did not know what it was that was sullying my spirit. When those close enough to me would ask if anything was wrong, they would get my tried-and-true reply "I have a headache". But now I can say I *feel*. And more so, I am aware of what I am feeling.

It took a while, but I finally recognized and identified deep feelings of anger and of guilt. I thought grief was my biggest enemy. Grief was extra baggage I was carrying, but the bigger culprits were the feelings of anger and guilt.

Guilty Feelings

- Guilty for being born and trapping my father.
- Guilty for being born a girl.
- Guilty that I was the 'perfect' child and having my sister constantly compared to me.
- Guilty for not being as good as the son or daughter of my mother's friends.
- Guilty that I did not love my mother the way she wanted me to love her, or at least show it.
- Guilty that I did not move out with my sister.
- Guilty that I failed at my marriage.
- Guilty that I had problems conceiving.
- Guilty that I lost jobs when I should not have.
- Guilty that I was smart(er).

- Guilty that I did not do anything to prevent my father's death.
- Guilty that I put so much on George's plate because of my immobility.
- Guilty that I did not know what I was feeling and subsequently hiding.
- Guilty enough that I had to stage a happy go lucky persona so no one could suspect anything.

I am vocalizing, putting on paper the feelings which reside deep in my heart and soul. I do not feel like I'm writing a book, but rather I feel like I am getting in touch with my feelings and letting them spill out in words and in print.

CHAPTER 25

Mice?
Are ten-year-old supposed
to act like adults?

When I was three years old, the part of the city in which we lived had mice. Mice were not a strange sight in the neighbourhood. Nasty, unwanted, but common; no big deal. I remember one day my mom had baked an apple pie. Since my father worked nights, she left it in the oven for him to find when he got home. And when dad went to get a piece, he came face to face with a mouse who was having first dibs.

The area behind the house had a recessed yard where the janitor who overlooked the buildings hung her wash to dry. One day as I was looking out my bedroom window which faced directly onto this yard, I saw a mouse being chased by one of her cats. I was three years old. I thought it was all fun and games, like the cartoons I watched. The cat cornered the mouse. I watched as the mouse bounced from one paw to the other. And then, just like that, the cat killed the mouse. I was horrified. But I didn't make a sound.

To look out the window, I had to climb onto the radiator. I was not allowed to climb there. Yelling or making any sound would have given me away, and I would have been punished.

I was 10 years old when my parents bought their house. That house was built in the 1940s and its layout reflected the design of those years. The only access to the basement was from the outside. There was a door in the backyard that led to the basement. And it was more of a cellar than a basement. My dad decided to take apart a closet and build a stairway allowing access to the basement from inside the house. That opening not only gave us access to the cellar, but it gave the mice living there, access to the house. Yuk!

Dad was neither a carpenter nor a builder, but when we sold the house 50 years later, those stairs were still sturdy and strong.

We had half moved in. Dad had set mouse traps in the basement, right by the stairs. To get up into the house, the mice would have to somehow bypass the traps. Fortunately, they were not that smart.

One day, friends of my parents dropped by unexpectedly (a normal occurrence at our house). Dad asked me to go downstairs to get a couple of folding chairs. I don't know at what speed I went down the stairs, but I do know I came back up at turbo speed. I had come face to face with a mouse held down by one of the traps. I did not say a word. I did not want the guests to know. I was being polite. I was being mindful and keeping the fact that the house had mice, a secret.

Dad had only to look at my face; he understood at once. He went to the basement for the chairs. Later, when the guests left, he tended to the traps. It was then that I heard him tell my mother what had happened. They were both relieved that I had not screamed.

Mice, hamsters, and all other furry varmints still give me the heebee geebees. In biology (years later) I had no issues dissecting worms and frogs. But rats .. No Way!

CHAPTER 26

Positive energy

"Know your worth.
Don't lower your standards."
..... (this one is mine ☺)

People often tell me how they love my upbeat and inspiring attitude. I am often told that I have a great outlook on life and great energy. And although I have my share of difficult times, I admit, I am fun to be around.

I have heard that life is a series of choices. I do believe that to be true, but only in part. I don't think anyone actually chooses to be born in poverty, or in a war-torn country. And I do not know of anyone who purposely chose to contract a serious illness, or to lose a limb, a mate or a job. So, are certain things we are experiencing a karmic debt or a contract we drew up in a previous life or dimension? Is that even possible?

There are several aspects and areas of our life for which we have choices. We choose our friends, what we want to wear, what we want to eat, what books we want to read and what movies we want to watch. It is also up to us to choose how we face the day. I choose to find the good in things, in situations and in circumstances.

Whereas I cannot control my illness, I do not and will not give it reason to make my life miserable. I refuse to give away my power to be happy. And so, I find reasons to be as joyful and as grateful, as often as I can.

I make a point of journaling three things daily, things for which I am grateful. Only three things a day, but I do so every day. I try *hard* not to repeat any of my entries. And I smile and try to bless everything in sight. Silently and to myself of course, I try to bless everything in sight. I purposely put myself in a loving and good mood. Just as I purposely apply makeup and perfume and jewelry to my body, I purposely apply happiness and gratitude to my soul.

I was not a flower child in the 70s, I have no intention of being one now. Wanting to be and feel happy is a personal choice. And if my disposition is pleasing to those around me, I am happy for them. We all have issues. If we can find even a few minutes of joy daily, then we win. I like winning. And I like winners.

CHAPTER 27

Emptiness

As cheerful as I am, there are some days that I feel completely empty.
I feel empty and lonely. Empty, lonely, and even useless.

I miss the ability to do what I want, when I want. I love company
and stimulating conversation. And I miss that. I miss my parents.
Whereas I miss my father's calmness and wit, I miss talking with
my mother. We did not often agree. In truth, we seldom agreed. But
we talked. A lot. About anything and everything. And we did things
together. We hit shopping malls, we went to shows, we traveled, we
argued, and we talked. She cooked and baked and while I watched
(and soaked in everything she was doing), we talked. I miss that. I
miss her. I miss my parents.

I miss getting into my car and driving places. I miss my independence. Thanks to wheelchairs and technology I can go to certain
places, even if those places are limited. But some days I still feel alone.
I feel so empty. I crave stimulation. I crave movement and excitement
and noise and laughs. I miss my life. I miss my legs and my independence. It's true, I am upbeat most of the time, a good deal of the

time. It doesn't just happen. I work at it. And fortunately, the more I work at it the easier it gets.

Still, there are times that I feel emptiness. Huge emptiness. The kind of emptiness that brings me to the edge of depression. And I have to be so very careful not to cross that edge. So, I get online and shop. Other times I surf the web to find stories which spark a reaction from me. And for a short period of time, I feel alive. Still other times I write. Or I sing. Loudly. Singing helps me forget the emptiness.

Everyone has feelings. Everyone has moods. Everyone has ups and downs, happy moments, and anger. These feelings and emotions are not reserved for or exclusive to the healthy or to the poor, to the educated or to those in love. For me and other who have limited mobility, we have our mind, our thoughts, and our memories to help us escape. In truth though, there is a limited number of times that memories can be replayed.

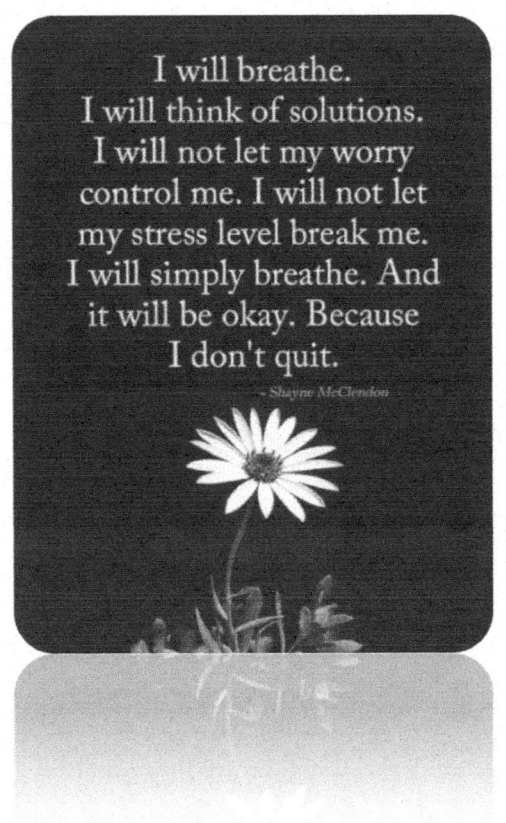

I will breathe.
I will think of solutions.
I will not let my worry
control me. I will not let
my stress level break me.
I will simply breathe. And
it will be okay. Because
I don't quit.

- Shayne McClendon

As I mentioned I crave conversation. And I am very aware that there are groups and associations which encourage people in my condition to discuss their feelings, to open up and let it out.

Thank you, but no thank you. There are those who have accepted their circumstance, totally content with their limitations. There are those who have given up. And there are whiners. My brain, my essence is the same today as it was 20 years ago. The only thing that has changed is my mobility. When I was perfectly healthy, I had ups and downs as do most people. I did not seek associations then. So why would I now? The only thing different about me today is lack of mobility. I am still me!

I have run out of things to say. For now, anyway. And in the months (and months) that it took me to write what turned into this book, something has changed. I have recognized, acknowledged, and dealt with a lot of memories and feelings. I have stopped dismissing things which bother or irritate me. I speak up, and I speak out.

I cannot leave you with words of wisdom. But I can thank you for allowing me to tell you my tale. So, when you see me in the wheel-chair, remember, *there's more to me!*

> *"One day you will tell your story,*
> *of how you've overcome*
> *what you are going through now.*
> *And it will become part of*
> *Someone else's survival guide."*
> .... *Brene Brown*